"IT'LL BE ALRIGHT ON THE FLIGHT!"

Humorous stories from three decades of wildfowling

By

VINCE RAW

This book is copyright. Enquiries should be addressed to Vince Raw. c/o Galloway Cottages Publishing, Stronord, Newton Stewart, DG8 7BD, Scotland. e-mail gallowaycottages@aol.com.

©Vince Raw 2000

First edition 2000, produced as a Limited Edition of numbered copies. Second edition 2003

The right of Vince Raw to be identified as the author of this work has been asserted in accordance with the Copyright, Design and Patents Act 1988.

All rights reserved. This book is sold subject to the condition that it shall not be reproduced, stored in a retrieval system or transmitted, in any form or by any means, electronic, photocopying, recording or otherwise without the prior written permission of the author. Nor shall it by way of trade or otherwise be lent, resold, hired out or otherwise circulated without the author's prior consent in any form of binding or cover other than that in which it is published.

ISBN 0-9539086-2-3

A catalogue record for this book is available from the British Library.

Line drawings and cover illustration by D. Lines-Edwards.

Published by Galloway Cottages Publishing.

Printed and bound by J W Arrowsmith Ltd., Bristol.

CONTENTS

Preface	5
1. First trip to The Wash	7
2. First trip to Islay	28
3. The Greg	51
4. Tony Wallace	58
5. First trip to the Ouse Washes	67
6. First trip to Pontoon Wash	93
7. Second trip to Pontoon Wash	110
8. A trip to the Solway Firth	131
9. Meeting Sid	159
10. A week at Wigtown Bay	167

The cabin on Pontoon Wash

PREFACE

The urge to go wildfowling all started when I was in bed with the flu reading the articles in the shooting magazines. I was twenty-three years old and full of the hunting instinct that somehow got into my genes. I blame it all on the articles I read, exciting and convincing me that there is so much pleasure lying in the mud in the middle of the night, on some wild foreshore in Arctic conditions. If I had any sense at all I would have used the magazine to light the fire with the next day, forgetting all about the articles. Unfortunately, this lunatic has very little sense which will become apparent if you decide to read on into a life filled with mishaps and disasters.

During my shooting years I have met some wonderful characters. Some, whom I am pleased to say, have still remained my friends. They have joined me on many wildfowling holidays and expeditions. There have been so many wonderful moments, exciting incidents and hilarious situations that I feel the need to write this book, purely to put things on record before I go to the foreshore in the sky to answer for all my sins.

The first story was when I was a young man, green behind the ears but as keen as mustard, venturing out to try and shoot my first goose. In the following stories I have introduced some comical characters that played a major role in my wildfowling education. Today, three decades later, I still have the same obsession and passion for wigeon flighting, although, more often than not, I leave the gun at home and take a camera. With Meg, my faithful spaniel sat beside me, I still marvel at the spectacular show of geese flighting off Wigtown Bay at first light. I consider myself extremely fortunate living next to the bay. When I am too old to venture out, I will still be able to witness the geese flighting, looking through the window from the comfort of my bed.

Apart from the sport on our shooting trips, I always enjoyed the company and the humorous situations. Of course, things rarely worked out as planned, hence the title of the book.

ACKNOWLEDGEMENTS

Vince Raw would like to sincerely thank the following for their help and co-operation relating to this book.

Jennie Raw, for her company, patience, help and encouragement.

D Lines-Edwards, for the interest and tremendous enthusiasm in producing the illustrations.

Tony & Pat Wallace, for their friendship and memory contributions.

Ian Keith & Sid Taylor, for being involved in the stories.

J W Arrowsmith Ltd, for their help and kindness with the printing of the book.

Meg, my faithful spaniel, who sat beside me while I wrote it.

**Dedicated to: David, Jacky, Stuart and the late Michael.
My children, who shared my attentions with the wildfowl.**

"IT'LL BE ALRIGHT ON THE FLIGHT!"

CHAPTER 1

First trip to The Wash

I kept reading the wildfowling stories in the shooting magazines. I had even joined W.A.G.B.I. (Wildfowlers Association of Great Britain & Ireland). There were several magazines in which guides were offering their services for goose shooting on The Wash. At that time I was working for an Irish man called Danny Murphy. We shared a shoot at Hemel Hempstead, renting the shooting rights from the Forestry Commission. I told Danny about my yearning to have a shot at the geese and it turned out he was keen to try it as well. Making a telephone call to a guide I booked three days for the two of us. The guide arranged accommodation in a pub in a small town near The Wash and we were to go in a couple of weeks' time.

I was so excited, I couldn't sleep at night. After reading all the magazine articles, I was firmly under the impression that to shoot geese you must have a big gun. Something, I have since learnt, is a load of rubbish. My gun was a standard twelve bore with half and full chokes. A friend of mine had a great collection of guns so I went to see him to try and borrow something more suitable for the job. He insisted I took a side by side eight bore. It was a beautiful English gun with Damascus barrels. He also supplied some cartridges for it.

As the days passed by I bought myself new waders. I already had a pair of waders which someone had given to me. I had never used them as they seemed a bit tight, but I thought they would be useful as a spare pair. I also bought a new torch. Looking back, I think I have lost a torch on every foreshore in Great Britain.

I read an article on wildfowling in a magazine, where it described how to make a hide with chicken wire and reeds, making a sandwich of the wire, and the reeds being the filling. Thinking this would be useful I made one. I have used this on many occasions, but I must admit, it gets heavy after carrying it half a mile.

Sunday morning arrived and we loaded up Danny's Ford Cortina estate, managing to fill it with lots of things that we thought might come in useful. We didn't take our dogs as the guide had told me on the telephone, that dogs are more trouble than they are worth on the foreshore. Looking back at thirty-five years experience, I would say his statement was totally wrong. I would say a bad dog is more trouble than it is worth anywhere, but a well trained dog is an asset, wherever you are shooting.

We were on our way and a dream was about to be fulfilled. The atmosphere in the car was tremendous. I was twenty-three while Danny was well into his forties and we were excited like a couple of kids going to a birthday party.

Arriving mid afternoon we had little trouble finding the pub where our accommodation had been arranged. The problem was the pub was closed. Knocking on the pub door we received no answer so we decided to sit in the car for a while as someone would be bound to arrive. After all, they knew we were coming.

After sitting there for about an hour Danny was losing patience. Probably because we were hyped up, Danny got out of the car and banged hard on the pub door. It's a pity we didn't do that immediately when we arrived because it brought a response. Someone opened a bedroom window and enquired quite rudely, *"What do you want?"* I explained who we were and that we were booked in at the pub for accommodation for our shooting trip. The man looked angry and said, *"You are early, wait there and I will come down."* He came down, opened the door and invited us in. As I walked into the pub the first thing I noticed was how cold it was inside. I apologised for disturbing him and explained that we had not been given a specific time to arrive. The orders from the guide were, go to the pub on Sunday and he would see us there. The man, who turned out to be the landlord replied, *"It's all right for him to say that, but I need my sleep between opening hours and we don't open tonight until seven. Seeing as you are here I will show you your room and you can use the back door to bring your things in. Then I am going back to bed."*

Having lived in lodgings for a part of my life, I have seen some dodgy places, and met some strange characters, but I must admit, I did not expect this. He showed us to a room on the first floor at the front of the building. It was a small room with two single beds and a chest of drawers. The room smelt damp and musty. The window had nine small panes and one of the small openings had half the glass missing. I thought to myself, hardly the Ritz but it will do. After all, we are here to shoot geese, and not laze around in luxury.

In the couple of hours waiting for the pub to open we looked around the small town. It was like going back in time. After the hustle and bustle of Bedfordshire this was like another planet. I like peace and quiet so it didn't really bother me, it just surprised me.

When the pub opened at seven we had a pint with the landlord. He was much more civil after his sleep. The place was freezing and it just seemed to be getting colder. The guide still had not contacted us and we were concerned. I mentioned this to the landlord. He said he would ring him, which he did. The reply from the guide was, he couldn't come tonight but he would meet us in the pub car park at six in the morning. With that message the butterflies started all over again and I temporarily forgot about being frozen. However, Danny hadn't and said, *"Let's get out of this place or I am going to suffer the same fate as the brass monkey."*

I didn't need persuading. We walked down the street looking for somewhere to warm up. It was January so you would expect it to be cold, but in that pub, it was like a damp cold. It sort of lingered around your body looking for an unprotected orifice where it could enter. Probably to warm itself up.

We found another pub and went inside. Unbelievable! It was like walking back in time fifty years. There was a man playing the piano. He looked about a ninety-three and had a pint of beer on the top of the piano which was swishing around in the glass while he was enthusiastically bashing out some tune I had never heard before. Probably written in the eighteen hundreds but more than likely, he was making it up as he played it. There were a couple of men standing at the bar with cloth caps on. They gave us the kind of look that meant, *"Here come another two bloody goose shooters."* The man behind the bar smiled and said *"What can I get you gentlemen?"* Danny ordered a pint of beer. I was so cold I asked for half a pint of beer and a brandy. His reaction was amazing. He got so excited when I asked for a brandy I thought he was going to wet himself. I don't think he had sold a brandy in the last ten years. The atmosphere was better in this place and after half a dozen brandies I started to feel warmer. At half past ten they closed the bar and we rushed back to the pub where we were staying, before we were locked out.

The landlord said he would have our breakfast ready at nine the next morning and wished us good luck with the shooting. After saying goodnight we went upstairs and walked into the bedroom. It was like walking into a fridge. Hurriedly, we got into our pyjamas and into the beds which was like climbing into a wet sack. The person who had been in my bed previously, must have been so cold that he lost control of his bladder and deposited the contents into this mattress, which could only be described as a wet sponge that didn't smell too good. There were slates missing off the corner of the roof. The water must have been coming in for a long time because the plaster in the corner of the ceiling had fallen away. That was the first time I had ever laid in bed looking at the stars with the curtains closed. About four in the morning a motor bike roared past. The room shook so vigorously I honestly believed for an instance that it had been ridden between the beds. I lay there unable to sleep and started to think of our shoot at Hemel Hempstead.

The shoot comprised of just sixty acres of young trees. There were rides and tracks running through it dividing it up into small manageable sections. The trees varied in height from three to six feet. Two or three guns could spend a steady five hours slowly working the sections. A paradise for the dogs. We never shot large bags, usually fifteen or so pheasants.

Adjacent to our shoot was a very large estate which employed two gamekeepers. They shot once a fortnight dividing the estate in half so each half was shot once a month. It was separated from our shoot by one small field. I heard that they reared and put out about five thousand birds. Me and Danny managed one hundred and fifty. I could see the pheasants in great numbers wandering out into the field during the day on the opposite side. I decided that they wouldn't miss a few of their pheasants and started scheming, trying to think up a plan were I could encourage some of the pheasants onto our shoot without breaking the law. One evening when it was quiet, I walked over to the other side of the field where I knew the pheasants would be scratching around the next day. I threw some wheat about and then laid a trail of wheat back across the field into one of our small woods. That should do it I thought and went home feeling pleased with myself.

Wrong! The luck of the Raw struck and things couldn't have gone worse. I forgot to put some directional arrows out along the side of the trail. Instead of the pheasants from the large estate coming over to join our birds, our stupid birds went across to join them, and stayed there.

Some times our shooting day would correspond with that on the estate. Apart from the fact that I was envious watching our neighbours shoot, I also noticed that we didn't put up as many birds as we usually did. I was starting to wonder if this was just a coincidence, or was there a good reason for it. I decided I would keep an eye on things next month when they shot again.

On the day of the next estate shoot I was in one of our small woods before daybreak. I really enjoyed watching the day break. Among the animals I saw was a beautiful fox. He sat down and washed himself no more than thirty yards from me. I know if you want a successful shoot you should shoot the foxes. I did shoot a fox once and vowed I would never do it again. I couldn't get it out of my mind. To me it was like shooting a dog. If the fox is going to steal ten pheasants in a season I would rather put ten more down on the shoot than shoot the fox.

Half an hour after daybreak I saw some pheasants flying out of one of our small plantations and across the field into the estate. These were soon followed by more and then it became apparent why. I could see the two gamekeepers from the estate meticulously working four Labradors through our sections driving everything over to the estate. They were waving white bags at any bird which wanted to fly back. I moved quickly towards them keeping out of their sight. As they came out onto one of the tracks I was there waiting for them. They looked horrified when they saw me. I told them who I was and that I knew who they were and what they were doing. One of them said the only reason they were there was because a fox had ran into a large bunch of pheasants on their shoot earlier that day and frightened them across. They were just flushing them back because they were shooting later. I told them I knew they were shooting later. That's why I was there and that I had been there since long before day break and I had not seen a pheasant fly in from their woods. The other keeper had said nothing up to now and looked rather uncomfortable. Walking over to me he forced a smile and said, *"Look! surely we can sort this out. It isn't what you're thinking, we did come to push our birds back. To make up for this misunderstanding how would you like to join us today for some driven pheasants?"* I thought for a minute. Our pheasants are only one field away and I am sure I can encourage them back along with a few of theirs. I don't think they will try this stunt again so why not take advantage of the situation. I told them I would accept if they would extend the invitation to two.

Me and Danny had a wonderful day's shooting. The keeper told the captain that we were his friends and that we were going to make a television documentary on shooting. The captain must have desperately wanted an appearance on television because he put us on the best pegs. The birds were high and fast and I shot well.

I did manage to encourage our birds back where they belonged the following week but I had better not say how.

Half past five seemed to take forever to arrive and I was pleased to climb out of the swamp. We quickly got dressed, collected the guns from under the beds, which we had been cautious enough to wrap in polythene, and proceeded down to the car park to meet the guide. It was a good ten degrees warmer in the car park than it was in the bedroom. The guide arrived half an hour late at six-thirty, just as we had started to believe that he wasn't coming. He was in a van that should have been taken off the road twenty years before. I was pleased when he instructed us that he would come in our vehicle and leave his van in the car park. However, it did create a problem. The back of the estate car was full of things we thought might come in useful. Pity we never thought of a dry bed! I scrambled on top of all our luggage and the guide got in the front with Danny. He was a tall hard looking character. A man of few words. Just about everything he said turned out to be an order. Following orders of, left here, right here and so on, Danny was eventually told to stop the car. The order then was, *"Get your guns and follow me."*

I started to get the hide from the car only to hear the stern voice saying, *"You won't need that now. Hurry up, we are late."* I decided not to say, I wonder whose fault that is. It was pitch black so I put the torch on to see where I was walking, only to be reprimanded again, *"Put that bloody torch out. Can't you see in the dark?"* I didn't have the courage to say no. Stumbling on behind I was tripping over tufts of grass and slipping about on the mud.

After what seemed like a two mile blind hike, we left the tufts of grass behind and concentrated on pure mud. It was getting deeper and deeper. I could hear Danny puffing and blowing and I was beginning to wonder if it had been wise to drink so much brandy the night before.

We walked for a long time crossing deep wide channels and the mud got worse. If only I had been allowed to use my torch I am sure I wouldn't have fallen over so many times. Eventually I could hear water and realised we were heading down to the shore line. The pitch black was now beginning to recede and I could just about make out the layout of the land. Day was now breaking, yet on we went through the mud until a sudden shout from the guide, *"Get down wherever you can. They are coming."* He grabbed Danny and said, *"You come with me."* They both ran back the way we had come. I started to look for a gully to get into but alas there were none. We had crossed about thirty on the way but now the mud was as flat as a pancake. I wasn't sure what to do when the guides voice bellowed out, *"Get down or they will see you."* I flopped down on my knees and started to sink into the mud. That was when I heard the most magical sound I have ever heard in my life. Although there were no geese to be seen, I could hear them. They must have been just lifting up from their roost. I was struggling to get the eight bore out of its sleeve and all the time the noise of the geese was getting louder and louder. It seemed as though the sound was in stereo. All around me I could hear geese calling. I didn't know which way to face. The calls from the geese seemed to be everywhere.

The day was breaking quickly when I got my first glimpse of the geese. A massive skein way out over the water flying parallel with the water's edge. The noise of geese calling went on around me but the only geese I could see were passing across some half a mile out. Suddenly, the skein turned and were heading straight towards me. My heart leapt into my mouth. I had never had a shot at a goose before, never mind three or four hundred. I was terrified and saying to myself please don't come over me, please turn away. On they came calling in excitement as only geese can. Still the geese were shouting behind me. I turned my head but I couldn't see a goose there. The skein was now getting close, probably about forty yards high. I was terrified and shaking. I just didn't know what to do. That was when my inner voice started to have a go at me. It said, *"What is the matter with you Vince? You have read about it, talked about it, dreamt about it, paid money to be here, slept in a freezing swamp to be here, you have the right gun for the job, the geese are here, for Pete's sake for once in your life have some confidence, put up the bloody gun up and shoot one."* Bugger it! I will. I was knelt in the mud, bent right over to be as inconspicuous as possible. The geese were just out in front of me and the noise was deafening. I remembered reading that if you shoot at a goose and miss it, there is a good chance you will hit the one behind it, so always take a bird at the front of the skein. I straightened my back and threw the eight bore up to my shoulder. I swung through the third goose from the front of the skein and fired. It was like a cannon going off and I missed. The recoil of the gun pushed me another three inches into the mud and I lost my balance making it impossible to fire the second barrel. Our guide who, I now realised, had settled in a gully some twenty yards behind me, blew his top. He was screaming, *"You shouldn't have fired until I had fired. I always fire first."* I remember thinking, a fat lot of use you telling me this now. After the shot had been fired, the skein were in total panic. The birds at the front climbed up vertically while the birds on the flanks split into two groups. The ones on my left turned back to the sea and the ones on my right swung out about a hundred yards and then carried on inland. Six shots rang out and two of these geese dropped from the sky. I heard the guide scream, *"Get down and keep still. There might be some more and don't bloody well shoot until I do."* I huddled down onto the mud which by now was pouring into the top of my waders at the back. Another three skeins came along the water. Still I could hear geese close behind me but I dare not look. I was in enough trouble as it was. The three skeins carried on along the water and came off a long way to my left. I heard a couple of shots in the distance but I didn't see any birds drop.

It was now full daylight and the flight was over. I heard the guide shouting again, *"You shouldn't have fired. You ruined it for everybody."* I thought to myself, what is this fool on about now. What does he mean I have ruined it for everybody? There was only Danny and myself. The guide was being well paid so he shouldn't expect to shoot. I decided I had taken just about enough from this idiot and I was going to tell him. I struggled to my feet and when I turned around I gasped with horror! I couldn't believe my eyes. There was the top half of the bodies of about a dozen men sticking out of the mud and spread out just thirty yards behind me. They were standing in gullies and every one of them was glaring at me. The reality of it all suddenly hit me. These people must have been experienced wildfowlers. They had probably watched the geese on Sunday morning to determine where they were likely to flight off and had come out early this morning to find a suitable place to wait where they could stand up to shoot when the time came. They had been calling the geese in. Hence all the noise behind me. Can you imagine what they thought of this lunatic perched out on the mud in front of them with no cover and nowhere to hide? When the first skein came off the light was still dim so the geese obviously didn't see me but the other three skeins must have seen me. I stood out like a sore thumb. There were many remarks thrown at me but I kept my head down and headed back the way we had come. I could see people to our left wandering around trying to find the two geese that had dropped. I thought to myself, a dog would be useful there.

"You shouldn't have fired. I always fire first!"

In the car on the way back to the pub the guide kept on and on about it. He kept saying, I shouldn't have fired until he had. If he said it once he must have said it twenty times. I remember thinking, if he doesn't shut up I am going to loosen a few of his teeth, just to give him something else to think about.

The truth of the matter was, the guide knew it was our first trip and we were green behind the ears. He never turned up on the Sunday to brief us. He was half an hour late in the morning, which created the situation in which we were so late getting into position, that I didn't have a chance to find a suitable gully to hide in. I fired the shot that caused all the trouble but it could have been avoided if he had offered some friendly advice, prior to taking us out. I was quite upset with the situation. Looking at it now some thirty-five years later, maybe I shouldn't have been. From what I have seen of wildfowlers I would say ninety percent of them would have fired the shot, experienced or not.

We arrived back at the pub at quarter to nine. The guide went off in his van leaving instructions to be in the car park at quarter past two. We were going to shoot some wigeon on evening flight. That cheered me up a bit and I set about cleaning up the eight bore. Taking a blanket out of the car I laid it on the pub car park. Carefully dismantled the parts of the gun I laid them on the blanket. If my friend could have seen his eight bore now he would never have spoken to me again. I started to wipe off the mud with some tissues we had in the car. It took a quarter of an hour to complete the job which just made us right for breakfast at nine.

We were hungry. The last time we had eaten was lunch time the day before. We went into the pub through the back door. It was like the Mary Celeste must have been. Not a person to be seen. We had seen a café when we were looking around the town the previous afternoon. It was closed then but surely it will be open now. We waited ten more minutes. Still no sign of life so we went to the café. Thank God it was open.

We got stuck into a good fried breakfast with extra toast and two mugs of hot tea. At quarter past ten we went back to the pub to see what salvage work could be carried out on the gun cases and my waders. When we walked in the landlord greeted us, *"Good morning boys you are late! Never mind, I have kept your breakfast warm."* He showed us into the kitchen where a table was set for two. He said, *"You can't beat a good breakfast after morning flight. Sit down and I will get it for you. It is in the oven."* I was waiting for Danny to say something and he was waiting for me. We didn't have the heart to tell him we had eaten so we sat down and proceeded to eat another breakfast. Every time the landlord turned his back Danny transferred more of his breakfast onto my plate. I didn't want it any more than he did but I didn't want to offend the landlord by leaving it. The landlord said, *"Did you get a shot this morning?" "Yes"* I replied, *"but I got into trouble with the guide because I fired first." "Oh! you would"* he said, *"he always fires first. Didn't he tell you?" "Yes"* I said, *"about fifty bloody times but they were all a bit too late."*

After breakfast we went to the car to relax. We decided we could not spend another night in that room so we were going to look for a better hotel or pub. There must be something better not too far away. Our plan was, we would have a couple of hours sleep in the car, go to evening flight and shoot some wigeon, then go back and tell the landlord we were leaving. We would then find a warm place to stay with dry beds.

With bellies full of egg and bacon and being totally knackered, it did not take long to fall asleep. I woke at quarter to one and Danny was still asleep. I woke him and we walked around the car park to try and get the circulation back into our legs. While we were getting dressed for evening flight it was noticeable that the weather was getting colder with a wind that was cutting. There was more mud in my waders than on them and I thought it would be better to wear the spare waders I had brought. I decided to take my twelve bore for the wigeon and worriedly left the eight bore under the bed deciding it would be safer there than in the car.

Our friendly happy guide arrived ten minutes late and off we went again. Danny followed the directional instructions and I lay in the back of the car and said nothing. The road we were on was parallel to the foreshore. Danny was instructed to park on the grass verge, which he did. I looked at the clock in the car as we got out. It was twenty to three. The wind was howling and it was bloody cold. I had read about wigeon shooting and from what I had read, the windier it is the better the shooting. I was convinced my luck was changing and this was going to be one of those memorable flights, like the ones written by people in shooting magazines. With my twelve bore on my back and fifty cartridges in my pocket, I followed Danny and the guide down some steps in the sea wall and onto the muddy foreshore. In some of the articles I had read about wigeon flighting the bag was sixty to seventy birds. I was beginning to wonder if I would have enough cartridges.

We walked on in a line, the guide in front, followed by Danny with me at the back. I was trying to keep as much space as possible between me and the guide. I kept thinking, he doesn't realise how close he came to losing his teeth.

After walking for about twenty minutes, I began to realise why I had been given these waders. The right one had a sharp lump in the sole which was cutting into my foot and the left one seemed to have a severe kink in the rubber, just where it passes the little toe.

Never mind, I thought, it can't be much further now and carried on marching. I had to smile as it reminded me of Dads' Army.

After a while we came to a flash and proceeded to walk around it. The guide became quite active and excited now pointing to the ground every three or four feet shouting, *"wigeon shit, wigeon shit."* Well, we went right around the flash and the call of *"wigeon shit, wigeon shit"* was shouted at least thirty times. While I was following him around this guided tour of wigeon shit, I was looking for a suitable place to hide myself before the shooting started. I wasn't going to get caught out twice in a day. To my amazement the guide said, *"It's no good here. We will find another flash!"* Dads' Army set off again. Oh well, I thought, I am sure he knows what he is doing and limped along behind.

He seemed to be walking faster and I was struggling to keep up. I was convinced that his mind was like that of an athlete with the intention of wearing us down and then increasing the pace, thinking to himself, *"I will lose these two bastards in a minute and I will have all the shooting to myself."* By now, I was becoming paranoid with him and I had to talk to myself to calm down.

Thank goodness we reached another flash. He started the same procedure again. Another meticulous count of wigeon shit. Surely, I thought, this must be where we will be shooting. But no, after twenty minutes of carefully recording every piece of wigeon shit around the flash, we marched on yet again. I could now feel the blood slushing around in my right wader. I knew I had lost most of the skin off my little toe on the other foot and maybe most of the flesh. In bloody agony on I went. Yes, we soon stopped again to admire yet more wigeon shit. The only good thing out of this route march was, it proved that there must have been a tremendous population of wigeon here to produce the amount of droppings we saw.

We were marching again and it was getting darker and darker. God knows how many miles we had walked. I was becoming concerned as to whether or not I would be fit to walk back carrying fifty dead wigeon. It was getting very dark when we arrived at yet another flash and to my relief we were instructed to find some cover and keep still. I enquired, *"Do we wait for you to fire first?"* The answer came in his normal sweet tone, *"Don't be bloody stupid, shoot them when you see them."* Charming I thought, this man really enjoys his job.

Well, the gun was ready and the cartridges were in and I was excited. We waited and we waited. It got darker and darker until I couldn't see. I thought I was cold working on the East coast as an apprentice but this was the coldest I had ever been in my life. All my clothes were damp with sweat after the route march and they were beginning to freeze. If a wigeon had flown past me I would have been too cold to shoot it. I put my gun back in its sleeve and waited for the orders to leave. They were given about ten minutes later. I climbed out of my hole and stood there in disbelief. The guide then came out with the statement of the day, *"That was disappointing boys. I am not surprised though, there was no wigeon shit around this flash."* If I still had my gun out I swear I would have shot him.

We were marching back in the dark when the guide said, *"You can put your torches on now!"* I wouldn't give him the pleasure of telling him that I had lost my torch in the mud on the morning flight. I said, *"That's all right. I can see in the dark!"* and closely followed Danny's light. The pain in my feet was indescribable. Maybe you think I shouldn't blame that on the guide. Maybe you're right, but I could see the headlights of the cars on the road running parallel with the foreshore, two hundred yards away. We could have driven in comfort to the chosen flash with no wigeon shit. I was convinced that this was my punishment for spoiling things in the morning.

As we approached the car I caught up with Danny and said, *"Have you had enough of this yet?"* He replied *"Bloody right I have!"* I then said *"Are you ready for going home?"* He replied *"Bloody right I am!" "Thank God for that!"* I said, and that is exactly what we did. We arrived back in Dunstable in time for a couple of pints in our local. I told the story and our friends fell about laughing.

I have been on many flights on The Wash since that terrible day and am pleased to say some with considerable success. Not with the help of a guide I hasten to add, but with plenty of help from my Springer spaniel *Lisa*.

The next day I was in a traffic jam trying to get to work when I started to think about how I ended up being a builder. At fifteen I started working for a firm called 'Alma Jordon' as an apprentice bricklayer. I didn't enjoy the work very much because it was always so cold. Being situated on the East coast there is always a cold wind blowing in from the sea. The boss's son worked as a bricklayer and

I worked with him. The big bonus was he liked shooting. The boss owned a lot of land which he had acquired. Some was set out and planted for organised driven shooting but there was a lot of ground for rough shooting with a healthy population of partridge. The boss's son shot every Saturday afternoon throughout the season with four or five guests. Mainly walking up and surrounding fields that held coveys of partridge. I volunteered to do beating. Because I was prepared to do this for the pleasure and not for the money, I was welcomed. Ironically, one of the regular guest guns was my ex headmaster from when I attended Building College.

I really enjoyed being out in the countryside. The excitement of watching the dogs work and the shooting was something I had never experienced before. The biggest drawback was, there were a lot of hares on the land and after carrying four or five hares on a stick across my shoulders for several miles, I was exhausted. I can remember cycling five miles home after the shooting and being so physically drained, I was vomiting. However, my instincts were so strong that this did not deter me and I continued to go at every opportunity. I don't know where my hunting instincts came from. My parents had no love of the country and its way of life and none of my brothers or sisters have.

After a days beating I was often given a brace of partridges as acknowledgement for my efforts. I have treasured memories of sitting and eating a meal with my Mother. We would have a partridge each. My mother was an excellent cook and my mouth is starting to water just thinking about it. The rest of the family were not interested in sharing our meal. They didn't know what they were missing.

I think the boss's son appreciated my efforts beating because after two years it was suggested that I could occasionally take a gun. This created a major problem because I didn't own one. I asked my Mother to approach my Father to try and obtain his permission for me to buy a shotgun. It would have been a waste of time for me to ask him. My Mother's love of partridge probably helped because she was successful. I saved my money and bought an AYA Yeoman side by side twelve bore. My wages were four pounds a week of which I was allowed to keep one pound ten shillings. It took a while to save enough for a deposit but when I bought the gun, I was delighted. The gun was in a leather case and the cost was forty-seven pounds and ten shillings. If only I could have had a dog to go with it. Even my Mother's touch failed to move my Father on that subject. Even though I was prepared to pay for it, the cost of feeding the dog was always the overriding factor.

The boss owned a farm and during the Summer I was sent to help out with the harvesting. I was always given the job of carrying the chaff from the thrashing machine. The bloody stuff got everywhere. I can recall it even created a rash on my scrotum. Had I been lucky enough to be involved in any sexual activities, it might have given some concern as to what the rash was.

I enjoyed working on the farm and made friends with the farmer's youngest son, Tom. The farmer had three sons and they all worked on the farm with him. Tom was a couple of years older than me and enjoyed shooting. The farm was right on the River Humber foreshore. I would cycle fifteen miles on a Sunday morning with the gun on my back. Arriving early, I would help Tom carry out his duties of feeding and mucking out. Because I helped him, we would finish his day's duties by lunch time and spend the afternoon shooting. We shot vermin, and a few other things if nobody was watching. We would then go back to the farmhouse and have a meal with his family. It opened my eyes. I had never seen so much meat in my life. A great side of ham was produced and thick slices were taken off it. There was always a good fire and we would sit around it after the meal talking about farming and the countryside. I cannot explain just how much I enjoyed those Sundays. The fifteen miles back seemed to pass so quickly as my head was full of the memories of a wonderful day

The toilet facilities on the farm were something else. An outside toilet with a plank of wood for the seat. The thing that amazed me was, the plank of wood had two holes cut in it so two people could sit there side by side, and have a conversation while doing the necessaries.

My Mother's maiden name was Jordon, the same name as my boss. This was no coincidence, as she was my boss's cousin. My Grandfather was the brother of my boss's Father. The brothers were in business together as builders. My Grandfather stayed off work two days before Christmas and went to bed because he had the flu. My Mother, who was sixteen at the time, went upstairs to see her Father on Christmas Eve. He died from pneumonia while she was with him. He was forty-nine.

After the funeral was over, my boss's Father had a meeting with my widowed Grandmother. She was asked if she would like to keep a share of the business, as a sleeping partner, or would she prefer a cash payment in settlement of her deceased husbands share. She took the money. The business became extremely successful and the boss and his son were wealthy people with new cars. Because of my Grandmother's decision I have a bicycle. I think my boss realised the situation, because I must admit he was good to me. He invited me to a driven shoot one day. I really felt out of place. This was my upbringing coming out. My Father felt inferior to everybody and he made us feel the same. I was standing by my peg, with a doctor at one side and a judge at the other. With me, the apprentice bricklayer, in the middle. I shot reasonably well but not one pheasant that I shot was credited to me. They were all credited to the doctor and the judge. I had lunch with the guns but I would have been happier eating with the beaters.

The boss also owned Christmas tree plantations. Five weeks before Christmas every employee abandoned their usual work and went cutting Christmas trees. Casual labour was also used. Our means of transport to the plantation, which was about thirty miles, was a tipper lorry. It had a canvas cover over a steel tubular frame fixed to the back of the lorry. Benches were in the back to sit on. The weather is always cold on the East coast but at that time of the year it's bloody freezing. The wind howled through this canvas tunnel we were sat in. We stopped on the way to pick up the casual labour. They were all women. I would have preferred to have called them ladies, but most of them certainly were not. If I had ever doubted that I had lived a sheltered life, I had no doubts now. Some of the women were coarse, dirty and they smelt. They would willingly offer their body for a packet of Woodbines. An offer that was frequently taken up by one of the hod carriers.

Overtime was available as it was a seven day week cutting trees. Nobody seems to want a Christmas tree in January so it was get stuck in and get the job done. The first year I worked on the plantation, my rate of pay was one shilling an hour (5 new pence). The tradesmen were on five shillings an hour. On Sundays, we were paid double time which put the tradesmen's wages up to ten shillings an hour. The boss had indicated that he didn't like the apprentices working on Sundays. The foreman said, if I wanted to work on Sunday I would have to ask the boss nicely. I approached the boss and asked, *"Please Mr Jordon, can I work on Sunday?"* He immediately said, *"Yes, that will be alright,"* I said, *"Thank you Mr Jordon."* What a bloody joke! I was doing the same work as the men for a fifth of their wages, and had to beg to do it.

The foreman was in his mid twenties and a swine. When I started my apprenticeship he had just come out of the Military Police after his National Service. He had been made foreman and given three pence an hour over the flat rate. However, most of the employees had been working at the firm for years, and they took no notice of the young foreman's orders. This infuriated the foreman and he would take it out on me. I didn't like him and I was frightened of him. One of his favourite sayings to me was, *"Come here you snot gobbling little bastard."* A term of endearment if ever I heard one.

The boss had a big car. The foreman had a little motor bike and the rest of us had cycles. That was the way it was, and had been for years. There were no prospects of this ever changing, when you look at the wages that were being paid. I can remember cycling to work and there was a row of cyclists six deep and as far ahead as you could see.

It was two weeks before Christmas and all the trees had been cut, when I received a letter from my two eldest brothers. My brothers were bricklayers and had left home when they had finished their apprenticeships to try and earn more money. They had travelled the country living in a caravan, working piece work wherever the work was. Settling in Dunstable they had started a small building business. In the letter, they explained that they had signed a contract to build a house with a garage. The contractual agreement stated, the work had to be completed by Christmas. The house was nearly finished but they had not started the garage. Could I come to Dunstable for a couple of weeks to help them complete the work? The thought of travelling excited me. I had never been more than forty miles from Hull. I asked Mr Jordon very politely for some time off. To my surprise, he said I could take two weeks holiday, but was quick to point out that they were without pay. I was on the bus the next day with my trowel in my suitcase.

Arriving in the Square at Dunstable, after an eight hour journey, my brothers were there to meet me. They took me into a café and bought me beans on toast. It was great to see them again although I felt embarrassed eating in the café. I had never been in a café or restaurant before. I was still suffering from the inferiority complex that my Father had stamped on all of us.

The next day I went to work with them. The house they had just built was one of many on a large building site. There were several houses under construction but none of them appeared to be occupied, and yet, there were lots of nice cars parked in the road. I was confused and asked my brothers, *"Who owns the cars?"* The answer was, *"Oh! they belong to the bricklayers and joiners."* I was flabbergasted! Bricklayers and joiners have bicycles not cars.

We finished the garage a couple of days before Christmas and my brothers took me out to show me around Dunstable, introducing me to some of their friends. One of these friends was an Irish man called Jack Maroney. He employed a gang of bricklayers and hod carriers and worked on piece work (which has since been called the lump). While I was talking to him he offered me a job on eight shillings an hour. This was two and a half times what my wages were in Hull. I said I would let him know after Christmas as my brothers were going to Hull for Christmas and I was going with them.

We went home for Christmas in a car my brothers had hired. It was a new Ford Zephyr and it was beautiful. Although I had only been away for two weeks I was missing my Mother and during the car journey to Hull I was looking forward to seeing her. When we arrived home we were walking down the path when my Mother opened the front door of the house. I was in front when my Mother came rushing down the path to meet us. I was so pleased to see her but so hurt when she rushed past me to welcome my brothers. We had a nice Christmas. My Father worked Christmas Day of course, rather than be with the family. He didn't have to work Christmas Day every year. He just couldn't resist the treble pay being offered. A little bit more to save. Over the Christmas period I considered the dilemma I was in. What was I to do? A chance to earn big money, but it meant leaving my Mother. I went to see Mr Jordon and told him what had happened, and that I was considering moving South. Mr Jordon said I would be a fool to leave as he would guarantee me a job as a foreman when my apprenticeship was finished. What a wonderful prospect in life, I would be able to buy a little motorbike!

That statement just about made up my mind that I should move South but I wanted to discuss the situation with my Mother. I remember she was shocked when I told her what I was contemplating doing. I will never forget her statement. *"We have kept you and spent money on you for all of your school days and now you are bringing money into the house, you want to leave."* I remember muttering to her that I didn't realise I had been born as an investment, and promptly moved South.

After two years away I drove back to Hull in my new Vauxhall Cresta and parked it next to Mr Jordon's car. I will never forget the expression on the foreman's face.

I worked for Maroney and my brothers, on and off for the next six years, laying bricks. From eight in the morning until six at night. It was head down and arse up. We worked like lunatics averaging well over a thousand bricks a day. During this time I lived in digs and met some characters. The best digs I stayed in was a house run by an Irish woman called Mrs Ahern. The food was brilliant. There was so much egg bacon and sausage for breakfast, we would eat our fill and make our sandwiches for the day with what was left. Fridays were the only drawback. On a Friday morning the plate would consist of three fried eggs and nothing else. Mrs Ahern was a Catholic and the rule then was no meat on a Friday.

I shared a room with a man that was twenty years older than me. My bed was near the door where the light switch was situated and the other bed was at the other side of the room. In one of the other rooms were two characters who I became very friendly with. They were called Frank and Reg. They were from the North of England and extremely fast joiners, consequently, they were earning good money. The beauty of the piecework was the harder you worked the more you earned. The drawback was if it rained for the week you earned nothing.

Frank and Reg went to the pub every night, and in their wisdom they decided to take me with them and teach me how to drink. When I lived in Hull I went to the pub twice. The first occasion was a Thursday night to play darts with some friends. After drinking half a pint of beer I felt great. My friends suggested that I should go out with them again on Saturday night and I did. This time I had six pints of beer. One of the boys had borrowed his Father's car and he drove me home. He had to stop the car many times for me to be sick. When we arrived, he opened the house door for me and I fell in. I was lucky. My Father was on the night shift and everybody else was in bed. Going upstairs and climbing into bed I was feeling rather sorry for myself. Then it happened! My first experience of a room spinner. The bloody ceiling was rotating and I started to feel sick again. I knew if I didn't get to the bathroom quick there was going to be an awful mess on the bedroom floor. To get to the bathroom I had to go down the stairs, through the best room, through the living room, through the kitchen and into the bathroom. The luck of the Raw struck and I fell at the second hurdle. The best room was only used occasionally, usually Christmas. Its main function was a show piece for the neighbours, as it had a large picture window so people could look in, as they were walking past. In the room my mother had placed a wrought iron stand which held six flowerpots. These pots of course, were full of soil with plants growing in them. Well, they were until I collided with it. The plants went in all directions spreading the soil around. The carpet looked more like a flower bed. I didn't have time to try and rectify the situation, I had to get to the bathroom and quick. I was hanging over the basin in the bathroom when my Mother appeared. I don't think she could believe her eyes. Her best room in carnage and her quiet son totally leg-less. She exclaimed, *"Vincent, you are drunk!"* I tried to state that I wasn't drunk, but I was too pissed to speak. Well, my Mother being the person she was, cleaned up the mess and helped me to bed. She said, *"It's a good job your father is on nights. If he saw you drunk he would kill you!"* He never saw me but, when he came home in the morning he smelt it. He never spoke to me for the next six weeks. He would have liked to have killed me but my Mother talked him out of it.

The first night I went out with Frank and Reg I had two pints and was sick. I was ready to quit drinking at that stage but Frank and Reg insisted it was just a matter of your body getting used to it and then you will start to enjoy it, without being sick. They were right! After about three weeks of being sick every night, I arrived at the stage that I could drink two pints without being sick. Once this goal had been reached, they insisted that I should now be trying three pints. This I did and was sick every night for the next three weeks. I won't bore you with the rest of my drinking apprenticeship, but I was sick for about a year. After that I could drink ten pints and keep it down. Unfortunately, it's got to come out somewhere and I was up five times a night for a pee.

During this period of learning to drink, my room mate got fed up with me. Every night I would leave the light on. If I turned it off I was sure to be sick. His only hobby in life was playing with his bits under the bed clothes, and therefore, preferred the privacy of darkness. I don't think he realised I could still hear him in the dark. Every time he thought I was asleep he would get up and turn the light out. This inevitably caused me to feel sick and head off down the corridor to the toilet, switching the bedroom light on as I went. In the end it was agreed that I moved into Frank and Reg's room as it was a large room with a spare bed. It was a good arrangement. I could be sick every night, Reg snored all night and Frank wet his bed most nights and it never bothered any of us.

The author as a young man.

CHAPTER 2

First Trip to Islay

My first trip to Islay was with the Vicar. No, not the sort of man who spends half of his life wearing a frock, I don't have a lot of time for them. The Vicar is a nickname for a very good friend of mine called Ian Keith. We were close friends for years, almost like brothers. Unfortunately, Ian now lives in Devon and I live in Scotland. Consequently, we don't see a lot of each other. Ian has been to Scotland to see me on a few occasions and I have organised some shooting each time, but that's another story.

Ian Keith, The Vicar.

I was still inexperienced at wildfowling but learning rapidly. I had been to the Wash in search of my first goose three times but without success. It was now the end of the season so I would have to wait another year at least. While reading a shooting magazine I noticed an advert offering goose shooting in Islay. I started to get that dangerous feeling. The feeling that has cost me a fortune over the years. I really fancied the idea. Not only was it a chance to shoot my first goose but also a chance to see another part of Great Britain. I had never been to Scotland, never mind the Hebrides. I decided to ask Ian if he would like to join me for a week next season. The first question he asked was *"Can we stay in a hotel with a bar?"* I replied, *"Of course, the advertisement was placed by a hotel."* *"Wonderful,"* he said, *"it sounds pretty good to me."*

Ian had never shot a goose either. This of course was no surprise, he had never been goose shooting. He was a member of a small syndicate that I was running. We paid for the shooting rights on farm land and forestry at Leverstock Green near Hemel Hempstead. We reared pheasants in Ian's back garden and released them on the shoot. Ian wasn't a very good shot but that didn't bother him. To Ian, the social side to shooting was just as important as the shooting. I think if the truth was known the social side was more important. He was tremendous fun to be with. He always had a grin on his face seeing the funny side of everything. I must admit I do enjoy the social side myself. I have been known to take a good few drams in the pub during the post-mortem period after the flight. However, in my opinion nothing can beat the pure excitement of a good wigeon flight.

Both Ian and I had the expense of buying our own houses and raising our families. Spare cash was in short supply. We decided the best way to finance this trip was to save weekly. This we did by giving Ian's wife, Irene, five pounds each on a Saturday and she put it into a Building Society account for us. We booked in at the 'Port Charlotte Hotel' in Islay, for the second week of the following January.

The rest of the year was to drag a bit. I had just started my own building business. Mainly building extensions on existing houses. Ian ran a take-away food shop in Chiswick. He had to work long hours because the shop was open until two in the morning. He never complained and just got on with the job with a permanent smile on his face. On one occasion I was in the shop talking to Ian when a customer came in and asked, *"Have you got any soup?"* With a big smile Ian said, *"Yes, brown windsor or oxtail?"* The customer replied *"brown windsor please."* Ian lifted the lid off a stainless steel container and ladled some soup into a plastic cup. He then fitted a lid onto the cup and gave it to the customer. *"I am sure you will enjoy it sir, it's freshly made!"* Fifteen minutes later, another customer came in asking the same question. Ian told him the two soup options and the man decided on oxtail. Ian went to the same container and ladled out the soup. After the customer had gone, I said to Ian, *"You took the soup out of the same container,"* Ian laughed and said, *"Of course I did, there's only oxtail. They don't know the bloody difference!"*

    The pheasant shooting was very poor that year. I am pretty sure the majority of the birds were poached. There was a pond on the shoot which I fed. At first it was useless but I persisted with the feeding and eventually the duck started to come to it. The luck of the Raw struck again. The farmer decided to let the field next to the pond for some horses to graze on. Every time I went for an evening flight, bloody kids turned up to feed the horses. I would sit by the pond hoping the kids would go but the little buggers stayed until it was dark.

Christmas and New Year had passed and we had each saved the best part of two hundred and fifty pounds. The hotel and shooting costs were eighty, which left us a hundred and seventy pounds each to spend and that was exactly what we were going to do with it. I bought a new jacket, torch and six boxes of Alphamax number 1 cartridges. We were ready to go and I had planned our route. Straight up the M1, then onto the M6, through Glasgow, past Loch Lomond and on to Tarbett Loch Fyne. There we would stay in a pub for bed and breakfast and catch the ferry to Islay at six the next morning from West Loch Tarbett. Sounds simple doesn't it? With the name Raw, nothing is ever simple.

I had an old pick-up truck which probably wouldn't have reached the M1 junction in Luton so we decided to go in Ian's Volkswagen Beetle. It was kept in good condition as he needed it for work during the week travelling into London. The Beetle was somewhat restricted for luggage space but we somehow managed to get most of our stuff in it with a little basket on the back seat for my Springer Spaniel *Lisa*. When Ian and I were together we were never stuck for conversation. We had so much in common we could find something to talk about all day and with Ian being such a comedian we would laugh a lot too. We talked about work, our kids and their education, our wives (both were called Irene) and all the problems they caused us, interfering with our shooting instincts. Its unbelievable how a woman can't understand why a man would rather go shooting on a Saturday than go shopping with her.

We were going along nicely, halfway up the M6 when I asked Ian, *"How is the car for fuel?"* *"Getting low,"* Ian said, *"I will fill up in Glasgow. I'm not paying the ridiculous prices at the motorway service stations. The more money we waste on fuel the less we will have to spend on drink."* We both laughed and carried on our way. We were soon talking again about our shoot and some of the things that had happened on it throughout the season.

This season the land owner had increased the rent considerably. Rather than everybody having to pay more money, which we couldn't afford, we decided in our wisdom to take two more guns into the syndicate to cover the extra cost and raise a few more pheasants. I placed an advertisement and was inundated with replies. Quite a lot of the enquiries came from people who didn't have a dog even though I had mentioned in the advert that a good dog was necessary. We were to be firm on this. We had found in the past with a small syndicate, the man without a dog gets far more stands and this can cause problems. To be honest, if I didn't have my dog to take with me, I wouldn't bother going. I get as much pleasure watching my dog work as I do shooting.

We took on two brothers who lived about twenty-five miles away. They had dogs that turned out to be useless. The dogs must have been homosexual because they spent the whole day trying to mount the other dogs. The bitches had nothing to fear. I don't know where the pheasants disappeared to but we had several shooting days with very poor results. It was beginning to get embarrassing. My friends, who were the other members of the syndicate, accepted the situation. The two new members were starting to think they had been conned, or at least, that's what I thought they were thinking. Ian and I decided we had to bring a bit of excitement into the shooting day. There was a strip of woodland about two hundred yards wide. We put the two brothers on one side and I would go on the other side. Ian would walk through the wood with the other guns and dogs. The pheasants had disappeared from the wood. To make it interesting for the brothers, after working the wood for five minutes, Ian would shout *"pheasant to the left!"* I would wait a few seconds and then fire off two barrels. We did this a couple of times every shooting day. When the drive was finished we would get together and I would explain how I missed the damn thing. The brothers must have thought I was a lousy shot.

Three shooting days had passed and the brothers had not shot a pheasant. They had shot pigeons in Blackwater Wood along with a few rabbits and hares but not a pheasant. Ian and I decided on a plan. There was a small copse on the shoot that always held half a dozen pheasants but for some reason it was now empty. In the pen in Ian's garden were some laying birds and a few birds we had kept back because they were so small. Our cunning plan was to take some birds into the copse early in the morning on the next shooting day and leave them in the crate. When it was time to shoot the copse Ian would say, *"You all stand around the copse and I will go in and hunt it out with my dog."* While he was in there he would open the crate. The pheasants would fly out over the guns and the brothers would get a shot. Well, it all went to plan until the last bit. Ian went into the copse as planned. I placed the brothers in the perfect place and waited for the big moment. I thought, this will stop them thinking we have conned them when they see these pheasants screaming over their heads. The luck of the Raw struck. Ian opened the lid of the crate expecting the birds to fly out like racing pigeons when they are released. The bloody stupid things just hopped out of the crate and started scratching around. They were so tame that even the sight of the dog didn't bother them. I could hear Ian shouting at them. I couldn't believe my eyes when I saw four pheasants nonchalantly stroll out of the copse and walk between the two brothers. They even stopped to have a little scratch on the way to the main wood. I knew there were some more birds to come so I decided to go in and see what was happening.

The other birds had flown up a tree and were sat there preening themselves. One was hanging upside down from a branch like a bloody parrot.

We threw sticks at them but they seemed determined to stay put. I decided to fire a shot. That should move them! Well it did! One of the stupid things flew over the brothers and they shot it with four barrels. The other birds jumped out of the tree and ran across the field to the wood. We never saw them again. The brothers were delighted with their success but couldn't understand why all the other birds had decided to leg it rather than fly. Ian and I quickly moved everybody on to the next drive before somebody went into the copse and found the crate we had transported the pheasants in. We had a good laugh about it in the pub later.

We were still chatting and laughing when I noticed Loch Lomond. We had driven off the M6, up the A74 and through

"IT'LL BE ALRIGHT ON THE FLIGHT!" 33

One of them was hanging from a branch like a parrot.

Glasgow without stopping for petrol. I asked Ian, *"What's the fuel situation?" "Nearly bloody empty"* he replied, *"I forgot all about it."* We decided to carry on rather than turn back. We were bound to come to a garage soon.

After driving what seemed like miles with the petrol gauge on empty, we came to a village. Wonderful, there was a garage. Ian drove in and parked at the side of the two pumps but it was deserted. I went to the little kiosk only to find it was locked. While wondering what to do next I noticed that one of the pumps was automated. I read the instructions carefully. There was a flat piece of metal with a small ledge around it sticking out of the pump. On to this we had to lay a pound note then put the nozzle of the pump into the petrol tank and push the button. The pump would take the pound note and discharge a pounds worth of petrol. We followed the instructions to the letter. Placing a pound note on to the ledge and the nozzle into the tank I pushed the button. The flat piece of metal shot into the pump along with the pound note at about ninety miles an hour. It then shot out again empty, and that was that. No petrol in exchange. We tried again and the same thing happened.

What were we to do? We couldn't go on feeding our hard saved money into this pump all night. I noticed there was a hotel across the road. Going in I spoke to a very friendly man, who could well have been the owner. I told him what had happened at the garage opposite. *"Oh yes"* he said, *"this is always happening. Give me your name and address and I will see that you are refunded."* I thanked him and enquired if there were any more garages in the area. He told me to turn right at the next junction, there was a garage half a mile down on the right hand side. I jokingly said, *"It doesn't take pound notes does it?"* *"Oh no,"* he replied, *"it takes fifty pence pieces."* He changed a five pound note for fifty pence pieces and off we went again. We found the garage without any problems. The car was now running on a wing and a prayer because the tank was empty. After reading the instructions I put in fifty pence. Magic, the pump parted with some petrol. I put in another fifty pence and got nothing. The fourth and fifth fifty pence worked and the ninth and tenth. The bloody thing had robbed us but we were pleased to be on our way again. The rest of the journey went well and the roads were fairly quiet.

We arrived at Tarbett Loch Fyne at ten-thirty ready for a pint and a good sleep after a long journey. Tarbett looked beautiful with the street lights shining into the loch. Ian pulled up outside a pub. I said I would go in and see if it was suitable. We hadn't bothered booking in advance. At this time of the year we should have no trouble finding a bed. Wrong! As I opened the pub door I couldn't believe it. It was like the Yukon gold rush all over again. The place was full. There was music playing, women dancing and drunken men everywhere. I turned around and walked out. I had to go back and have another look. I thought I must have been imagining it. Unfortunately I wasn't. Going back to the car I said to Ian, *"I think they must have struck gold here, the bloody place is heaving"*. Ian suggested we try somewhere else. There was another pub up the road and I went in for a look. It was just the same as the other, if not worse. We have got to sleep somewhere I thought so I pushed my way through the crowds to get to the bar. Eventually I caught the barman's eye and he came over. *"Have you any accommodation for tonight?"* I shouted over the noise, he replied *"just one room with a double bed. It's got no basin and if you are for the ferry in the morning there will be no breakfast."* I didn't bother asking him how much the room was. I just turned and walked out. Ian and I are bloody good mates but a double bed is taking things a bit too far. I went back to the car and told Ian the situation. We decided we would find the ferry terminal and sleep in the car, I asked someone the directions to West Loch Tarbett. It was about two miles outside Tarbett Loch Fyne.

Our luck changed dramatically as we were driving down to the ferry terminal when we passed a cottage with a bed and breakfast sign outside. Ian stopped the car and I knocked on the cottage door. A little lady in her late sixties answered the door. I asked her if she could give us accommodation for the night. *"Are you catching the ferry in the morning?"* she enquired, *"Yes,"* I replied. *"We are going to Islay for a holiday."* She said, *"You had better come in. I have a room, as long as you are not working on that damned oil rig."* It was then I realised what was going on. This normally quiet village had been taken over by hundreds of people building an oil rig.

The cottage was warm, the beds were good and the breakfast was brilliant. I was given the biggest Loch Fyne kipper I had ever seen. We thanked the lady sincerely and took her telephone number. We were to stay in that cottage many more times over the years. A short drive and on to the *'Arran,'* a ferry run by *MacBraynes*. At six she sailed slowly out in the dark and we were on our way. I found it amusing that as soon as the boat had left the jetty, the shutters went up on the licensed bar. We decided that if you can eat kippers at half past five in the morning why not have a dram at half past six, so we did. It took about four hours on the ferry and we talked and laughed wondering what was in store for us in the week ahead. We were getting excited at the prospect of shooting a goose.

The ferry arrived at Port Ellen on Islay and we drove off. We were staying at Port Charlotte which was about twenty miles from Port Ellen. According to our map we had to drive over land to Bowmore, which is the capital of Islay. On this drive we saw Red Deer. Magnificent stags just a hundred yards off the road We then drove round the shore line of Loch Idaal stopping at least a dozen times. I had never seen so much wild life in my life. Every little bay along the shore was active with numerous species of ducks. When we stopped to look I remember saying. *"We can come down here tonight for evening flight, I have never seen so many duck."* Then we would drive on a few miles further and there would be another bay with even more duck in it. It was absolutely incredible. I was really getting excited now. My imagination was going wild. I don't think the dog could believe it either because her tail never stopped wagging. We were taking photographs of everything and spent hours getting to the hotel. When we finally arrived at The Port Charlotte Hotel, we got out of the car and let the dog out to stretch her legs. A man came out of the hotel towards us. He was a very smart man. Tall, well built and casually dressed. *"You must be the boys for the shooting!"* he exclaimed in a soft Scottish accent. *"My name is Andy. Welcome to my hotel."* I said, *"Yes, I am Vince and this is Ian and it's good to be here."* We shook hands. *"Come in and have some soup,"* he beckoned and started off towards the door. Ian said, *"I will just lock up the car because we have guns in it."* Andy replied, *"There is no need to lock up anything here my friends. Nobody on this island will touch your things."* It was then I realised the natives of this island live a different life than we are used to. We left the car unlocked and followed Andy into his hotel. If the guns had been stolen we would have been in trouble with the police for not locking the car. Although we had only just arrived, somehow I knew that nothing like that was going to happen. We sat with Andy and had some excellent soup along with a good pint of beer. He asked us about our journey. We told him about the petrol and the gold rush. He laughed heartily. I knew I was going to like this man.

    We talked about the dog and it turned out that Andy had two Springer Spaniels that were just six months old. We told him about the kipper for breakfast at half past five and how nice it was. He said, *"You will have kippers here before your bacon and egg."* Things were getting better! I told him that I was amazed at the amount of wildfowl I had seen on the shore and how I was looking forward to getting out there. The luck of the Raw struck again. He informed us that all the shore line was protected in Islay and nobody was allowed to shoot on it. What a body blow. He went on to tell us that he would take us out the following day (Sunday) and show us where we were allowed to shoot.

    After our lunch and a good chat Andy showed us to our rooms. They were first class! We brought all our gear up to the rooms, had a shower and slept until six. Dinner at six-thirty and the food was great served by a very friendly waitress. After dinner we went into the bar where we were to spend a great deal of time and money in the next week. We met some very interesting characters and Ian soon had them all laughing. The bar was fairly quiet until about twenty-five people came in just after ten. You could tell they had been drinking and they soon joined in with the fun. I asked

Andy why they should all arrive together. He told me that there was a pub in the village and these people had been in the pub until it closed. I asked him if it bothered him that these people had been drinking in the other pub and then coming to his hotel after it had closed. *"Not at all my friend,"* he replied. *"It happens every week. We prepare a basket meal for them and they stay in the bar until two or three in the morning."* We had a great evening with these really friendly people.

At nine on Sunday morning we went down for breakfast. As promised there was a kipper followed by a big fried breakfast. Enough to keep you going for the day. During the morning we had a look around Port Charlotte. It was a quiet little place. The main employment was a distillery. There were eight distilleries on Islay and we managed a trip round one of them. The majority of people lived in a croft with a few fields where they would run sheep. The Barnacle geese invaded Islay in great numbers. Sixty thousand a year according to one source. If they decided to feed on a crofter's field they could devastate the field in a day. The problem wasn't what they ate, it was the damage they did with their paddles. Apparently they would turn a pasture into a quagmire very quickly.

Sunday afternoon Andy took us out in his car to show us where we could shoot. He had a new Audi. Here was a tall intelligent man with a sense of humour. He owned a comfortable hotel and now we are in his brand new car. I must confess I was beginning to envy this man. There was a large area of ground we could shoot. Enough to last a day if we had wanted to walk it. He told us there were a lot of hares on the ground. When I was a teenager I shot a hare and injured it. The poor thing cried like a baby. I have never shot at one since. I asked Andy where we would be most likely to shoot geese and he showed us. While he was talking to us there were geese flying around. The excitement was mounting. On the way back Andy was telling us about the island and their customs. He had dinner with us and provided two bottles of wine on the house. I suggested to Ian that we should have an early night to be up in the morning with a clear head. Ian agreed and I finally managed to get him out of the bar at half past eleven. I lay in bed so excited I couldn't sleep and started to think of my childhood.

I was born and reared in Hull with two sisters and three brothers in a house that was not much larger than a cardboard box. My Father worked for most of his life in an iron foundry but his real love was the building trade. When he was in his twenties he worked as a plasterer's labourer soon realising there was no security in the job, when he was sacked on Christmas Eve. He decided to find a more secure job in a factory before he started his breeding programme with my poor Mother. My Father was a Catholic and believed he was sent on earth to produce offspring. He certainly believed that he was not allowed to enjoy the pleasures of the female body without making it pregnant.

When I was five I was sent to a Catholic school. There was a really good school with first class facilities opposite the house where we lived but it was Church of England. Consequently, I had to travel four miles on the bus to this other school which was run by Nuns. You must realise that in those days very few people had cars and therefore, most people travelled on buses. A small fellow in short pants had little chance in the vast queues at the bus stop early in a morning. This resulted in being late for school on numerous occasions, which probably meant, detention or no dinner. When I arrived at the school I was usually greeted by a Nun with a red face rushing towards me with habit flying and screaming, *"Why are you late, Raw?"* It was no use explaining that the bus was full, or there had been an earthquake, or the bus had caught fire, or the driver of the bus had died. All of these logical reasons resulted in the same punishment. I tried various lies until I hit on the correct answer. *"Why are you late, Raw?" "Before I came to school Sister, I attended Mass with my Father." "Good boy Raw, your Father must be a good man!"*

I spent the first two years at school learning how to make a confession correctly and being prepared to take my first Communion. Little time was spent on academic education. When I was eight I took my first Communion. This I was told would be the finest day of my life. On that morning the whole class was marched off to the Church to take Communion. The girls wore white dresses with veils and the boys wore trousers and shirt with a sash. We received Communion from a bloke in a dress, whom I believe was a Priest. We were then marched back to the school for a special breakfast that had been promised. After eating the damp cornflakes, we were allowed to go home early.

I will never forget walking into the house and seeing my poor Mother doing the washing over a tub. She was perspiring, pushing the washing up and down with a possar. (A copper bell shaped object that was full of holes and had a long wooden handle.) I remember feeling disappointed and cheated. What was to be the best day in my life turned out to be just the same as the rest of them.

My Father was satisfied he had done his duty by sending his tribe to this school. If only he had taken the time to go and see the school for himself. It was probably the roughest school in Hull. If you couldn't fight when you went, you soon learnt if you were going to survive.

My religious education continued and when I was eleven the school decided I was too stupid to pass an eleven plus examination. My Father whole heartedly agreed with the school's unwarranted decision. That meant, my chance of going to Grammar School had gone.

When I was twelve I heard that the Building College in Hull were looking for pupils. An exam had to be passed before acceptance. Writing to the college I was given the chance to sit the exam which I passed without too much difficulty. Wonderful! I had been accepted. A chance to get away from that dreadful school.

Eventually I told the news to my parents, not being sure whether they were pleased for me or not. I know they were not pleased about the fact that I had to wear long pants to go to the college and didn't own any. When my Grandfather died, his long pants were altered to fit my eldest brother. With the prospect of no immediate male member of the family about to snuff it, the other terrible alternative was to visit the pawn shop and see if they had any second hand long pants going cheap. One way or another I managed to obtain long pants and started my two year term at Building College.

The best part of attending school was being with my school friend Stephen Padgett. He started school the same day as me when we were five. He also passed the scholarship for Building College as I did. We were in the same class for ten years. He was a close friend and we had some wonderful times together. I only had to look at him and I would start laughing which usually resulted in trouble for me. When I was being reprimanded by a teacher, I knew Padgett was there grinning. I was terrified that he would catch my eye because I couldn't help myself. I would start laughing which of course infuriated the teacher and made the situation considerably worse.

Padgett had everything I ever wanted and I really envied him. He had a dog, a goat and pigeons and to cap it all his Father was an ice-cream man. My Father would not allow us to own any animals because it cost money to feed them. I used to fantasise about having my own dog and being out in the country side watching my dog working the hedgerows. I imagined being there with a gun with my faithful dog at heel. They were wonderful dreams.

I remember joining the scouts with Padgett. The first time we went the scout master was telling us what we were expected to do as good scouts, and all the time I was fighting back the laughter because Padgett kept looking at me. I managed to control myself until the end of the evening. We all went into a room and stood in a circle. One of the senior scouts stepped into the centre of the circle and started hoisting a small Union Jack up a broomstick, while the others saluted. Well, I looked at Padgett and we both burst out laughing and couldn't stop. We were kicked out of the scouts that night and we laughed all the way home. I realise now what a wonderful uniformed organisation the scouts are and I admire the people who run it. Often being a boy's first introduction to the outdoors and learning the ways of the countryside.

I lay in bed in the Port Charlotte Hotel smiling while thinking back all those years ago and finally dropped off to sleep.

The plan was we were to get up early. Andy had told us to go to the kitchen and help ourselves to tea and toast. When we returned from the mornings flight we would have our breakfast. We were up early full of anticipation. We went to the kitchen and were greeted by two very enthusiastic six month old spaniels. The house training of these dogs had not been very successful as there were quite a few mines lying on the floor. The silly buggers started tearing around wanting to play and they systematically ran through these little heaps and spread them evenly on the kitchen floor. We decided to clean up the mess before we went out. What a wonderful job at six in the morning on an empty stomach. After putting my dog and the guns in the car we were on our way.

It was about ten miles to the shooting area. The roads were poor and slippery with ice. There was no sign of grit or salt and the car was slipping about. I remember thinking, I hope the luck of the Raw doesn't strike and that we haven't come all this way just to end up in the ditch at the side of the road. Ian did a great job keeping the car on the road and we arrived at our chosen spot in plenty of time.

Walking across two fields there was a long row of gorse bushes about five feet high. We decided to stand in the bushes about fifty yards apart. I clipped my torch to my belt so I wouldn't lose it. A burn about ten feet wide was situated along the back of the bushes. The burn was behind me and Ian was to my right. Ice had started to form on the burn. I found a stick and pushed it into the burn to determine its depth. I was concerned about *Lisa* as she was a small spaniel. The burn appeared to be about two feet deep. Just enough for *Lisa* to get under the ice and not be able to break back through. I decided then that I would not let her into the burn. That spaniel was more than a dog to me. She was a very important member of my family and I wasn't going to take any risks of losing her.

It was still dark when I heard the first geese. They passed somewhere out to my left. I couldn't see them. I thought then if only we had set up a hundred yards further down we would have been under them. It went quiet again and the light was starting to break. I could hear geese again and they were noisy. I was straining my eyes to see them. They were getting louder and louder. Suddenly they were there. A massive skein of barnacles heading towards us. They swung one way and then back again. My heart was pumping so fast I thought it was going to burst. On they came swinging about filling the sky in front of us. As they approached us they swung to their left and passed Ian about sixty yards out. I thought Ian might be tempted to fire at them but he didn't. Five minutes later I saw a skein of twelve Greenland whitefronts pass about one hundred yards to my left and no more than twenty-five yards high. They slid over the hedge silently. Not a call from any of them. I was watching them disappear when I heard more geese. Another skein of barnacles was heading our way. A lot smaller than the first skein. These birds seemed quite content to fly in formation. They were coming straight at us about thirty yards high. This is it I thought. I started talking to myself drilling instructions into my brain. *"Don't shoot too soon. Don't move until you are ready to shoot. Make sure they can't see the dog. Pick a bird at the front and don't poke the bloody gun, swing it and remember to push the safety catch off."* I think the geese must have heard me talking to myself because they swung off to my right and crossed about twenty yards to the right of Ian. They were flying over the bushes when Ian fired. He connected with his first barrel. The birds split in panic and Ian missed with the second barrel. The goose he had shot dropped down in the field behind me but it was far from dead. *Lisa* looked anxiously at me waiting for the fetch command. I told her to stay. I could see the goose struggling to get away and decided I would go and retrieve it. I might not have shot it but it was our first goose and

I didn't want to loose it. I had waders on so I could negotiate two feet of water without a problem. Taking the cartridges out I laid my gun on its case in the bushes. Moving to the edge of the burn I tentatively pushed my foot in to find the bottom. The water came just above my knee and the bottom felt quite solid. I cautiously waded further out. The bottom seemed fine and the burn got no deeper. I had better hurry, I thought, or the flight will be over and I hadn't had a shot. The luck of the Raw struck. When I took the next step forward the flight was over for me. The bottom of the burn had disappeared. Straight down I went. The bloody burn must have been ten feet deep in the middle with a sheer drop. It's a good job my heart was thumping when I went under because it was so bloody cold I think there was a good chance it might have stopped altogether. I came up at the other side and dragged myself out. What a sight! I think even the poor goose must have been laughing. Ian certainly was you would have heard him two miles away. With waders, torch and pockets full up with water I set off in pursuit of the goose. I managed to catch it and dispatch it fairly quickly. I now had the goose but I was on the wrong side of the burn. *"Why don't you do breaststroke on your way back?"* Ian shouted. I screamed back, *"There's no bloody way I'm going in there again. I am going to walk up this side to try and find a bridge. Keep an eye on my dog and if you shoot any more geese, shoot the buggers out in front."* *"OK"* was the reply and I set off in search of a bridge. The field I retrieved the goose from was reasonably solid but the next field I came to was a peat bog. I was sinking up to my knees and the water in the waders was gushing out of the tops. It was then that my inner voice said, *"you have saved up all the year for this you must be round the bloody twist."* I ignored it and finally found a way across the burn. Staggering back I joined up with Ian and *Lisa*. Ian had a big grin on his face when he thanked me for fetching his goose. *Lisa* came to me and wagged her tail. She gave me that look that meant *"Serves you right! What do you think I am here for?"*

    The flight was over and we set off back to the hotel. There was a boiler room at the back of the hotel and that's where I headed before anyone saw me. Ian brought me a change of clothes and we went in for breakfast. When Ian related the story in the bar that night I must admit I had to laugh. He was describing it in great detail and enjoying every minute. He explained to his audience how he had shot this sixty yard goose stone dead and how I went to retrieve it. He said, *"He went carefully across the burn and when he reached the middle he disappeared under the water. His bloody hat floated past me and I was tempted to have a shot at it."* I have heard Ian tell the story many times over the years and every time the goose he shot got higher. My performance that day had left me tired and I was in bed at ten. I left Ian in the bar entertaining the locals as only he can.

The next morning we were up at five-thirty and in the kitchen for six. Concerned about the minefield we approached Andy's dogs differently. We didn't fuss them and we spoke to them in a stern voice. They were unsure about us so they stayed in their baskets. We easily cleaned up the deposits before they managed to spread them. We had missed evening flight the previous night because my waders were still wet inside but overnight the boiler had done a good job and dried virtually everything.

The weather had changed. The frost had gone and it was raining with a strong wind. We arrived in plenty of time. Andy had lent us some profile type decoys and we decided to put them out in the field fifty yards from the bushes where we would be standing. The ground was still hard under the surface and we had difficulty in pushing the decoy securing rods into it. We pushed them in the best we could and the decoy pattern looked all right in the dark. After taking up the same positions, Ian offered to change sides in case the geese came the same way. He genuinely wanted me to shoot a goose. I said I would stay where I was. I had the Greenland whitefronts in the back of my mind.

As the light broke the geese started moving. Skeins to both sides but nothing straight at us. I kept looking to my left and after a while there they were. A dozen Greenland whitefronts just twenty yards up exactly the same place as I saw them the previous day. Once again not a sound from them. I saw them disappear and thought to myself, *"tomorrow, I shall be waiting for you."* The barnacles were now moving in great numbers. After several skeins had passed us by I was beginning to think it was going to be a blank flight. As it became lighter I realised just how bad the decoys looked. Some had blown over at a thirty degree angle. Others had spun round in the wind. A couple were laying flat and one was blowing up the field. I decided to run out and gather them in. I am sure they were putting the geese further away from us rather than bringing them in. I ran out and grabbed them throwing them in the sack. I left the one that was blowing up the field. I was running back when I heard more geese. Diving into the bushes I nearly landed on my little dog. Spinning around I could see them clearly. Either they hadn't seen me or they had heard of my abysmal record at goose shooting because they were coming straight towards me. My bloody heart started again. I kept telling myself to relax and wait. The sight and the noise from these geese made me shake with excitement. There must have been fifty in the skein. I waited until they were just out in front. I was saying to myself, *"don't poke the gun, swing it."* I threw up the gun and swung through the third bird from the front. To my amazement it dropped stone dead from the skein. I was so overwhelmed that I nearly forgot to fire the second barrel. The geese turned away to my left and started to climb. I swung onto the last bird in the skein and it dropped about a hundred yards up the field. My little dog was sitting there frustrated. I sent her for the goose up the field because I wasn't sure if it was dead. She was back with the goose in no time at all and it was dead. I then let her fetch the first goose I had shot and gave her a big cuddle when she came back. It was worth all the misery I had been through. A few more skeins came but they were stretching range. We let them go by without a shot. I was using an over and under Miroku I had bought two years before. It had a single selective trigger. When I first used it I was forever reaching for the back trigger, which didn't exist, to fire the second barrel. I cured this by shooting a lot of clays through the summer.

    Breakfast was good that morning. I had the biggest grin on my face and there was no way it was going to leave me for a long time. We had a drive around Islay during the day. It was really enjoyable just to see so much wildlife compacted into a small island. We tried evening flight in the bushes at the same place. The barnacles all came back over us but about five gun shots high.

    Back to the hotel for a shower and dinner. An excellent meal which started with snipe on toast. It was the first and only time I had eaten them and quiet frankly for what is on the little things it is hardly worth shooting them. I have never shot a snipe and I vowed then I never would. After dinner we went in the bar. I felt elated after such a successful day and the booze flowed. It was half past one and Andy was still drinking with us. We were all getting worse for wear but I think I must have been the worst. When I asked for another drink Andy said he would only serve me if I could say ornithology. Well I tried my best with several attempts of *"orneeeth and hornath"* but there was no way I could get my tongue round it. After a while I told Andy, *"It's no good I can't say it, I will have to go to bed."* Andy laughed and enquired, *"can you say birds?"* I said, *"yes! birds." "That's close enough"* Andy replied, *"Have another drink."* I went to bed at half past two.

At six in the morning I was in the minefield drinking gallons of black coffee. When we went outside there was horizontal sleet blowing across the island and the roads were treacherous. We went back to our bushes but this morning I moved a hundred yards along to where I had seen the whitefronts cross. When it was breaking light the sleet stopped. It was nearly light when I saw the whitefronts. They were crossing the road where we had parked the car following the same flight line as the two previous days just twenty-five yards high. Surely I couldn't miss. They were gliding along without a sound. I waited until they were just out in front and threw up the gun. The luck of the Raw struck again. I pulled the trigger as I swung through my chosen victim and all I heard was a click. I desperately kept pulling the trigger but nothing happened. The geese didn't flinch. They didn't even realise I was there. The bloody cartridge had misfired. With the gun being a single selective trigger the second barrel is made ready to fire from the recoil of the first barrel. The result was simple, no recoil, no second barrel, no whitefront. I must have fired the best part of half a million cartridges and never had a misfire. What a disaster! It could only happen to the Raw.

In the afternoon we went for evening flight. The wind had picked up now and it was gale force. When we got out of the car there were lumps of foam the size of footballs blowing into our faces. The wind was blowing from the direction that the geese had flighted in the morning. We were in plenty of time so instead of going straight to the bushes we went in the opposite direction to investigate where the foam was coming from and maybe see where the geese had been roosting overnight. Crossing three fields, the foam was getting thicker. Eventually we reached the source. We were on top of a cliff edge with a sheer drop of about thirty feet. There was a vast expanse of water below, which we found out later was Loch Gruinart. The wind was stirring the water up into great waves. As the waves were blowing in they were crashing against the rocks below and great sprays of foam were leaping into the air. The wind was blowing the foam horizontally across the land. I wondered if the geese roosted out on the loch. If they did they would not be there tonight with these weather conditions. Getting soaked with the foam and spray, we did a hasty retreat back to our bushes. The geese didn't return to the loch but several mallard flighted over when it was nearly dark and we managed to shoot three of these. After returning to the hotel we discussed the tactics for the next morning with Andy. I was concerned that none of the geese had flighted back to the loch. Surely it would be a waste of time going back to the bushes in the morning. Andy agreed that I could be right, although, he commented that the weather can change very quickly and the geese could fly to the roost during the night. I asked him if there was another place where the geese might flight from. He said that if they don't return to the roost they might stay out on the fields and they could be anywhere. They probably wouldn't move until they were disturbed by a tractor in the morning so it was pot luck as to where they might flight. It was then that Andy came up with a brilliant suggestion. I had told him earlier of my love for wigeon flighting. He had told me that there were very few flashes on his ground that were suitable for wigeon flighting. However, he now told us that there was a loch where wigeon might roost during the day if the weather was rough and we might be lucky enough to get a shot at them coming in to roost in the morning. We agreed that the wigeon was the best option and Andy gave us directions to the loch. After dinner we had a few drinks in the bar. I wanted an early night as I was beginning to feel the pressure of a hectic few days and I was knackered. As we were leaving the bar Andy shouted *"You must come to the Ceilidh tomorrow night, you will enjoy it."* Lying in bed I was thinking about the wigeon in the morning. I was asleep in five minutes.

Out early the next morning we were enthusiastically trudging across peat bogs following Andy's directions to this fresh water loch. Although a strong cold wind was blowing, I was soaked with sweat when we finally arrived at the loch. There was very little cover at the edge so we set about making a couple of hides fifty yards apart. I crouched in my hide with *Lisa* beside me. It was very dark and it seemed ages before the first glimmer of light. I heard *Lisa's* tail start wagging. A sure sign something is going to happen. A flight of wigeon went over me so fast I never even got the gun to my shoulder. It was now a bit lighter and I heard two shots ring out from Ian. Almost immediately another flight of wigeon. I saw these a bit earlier and took one out. The speed these birds were flying was incredible. There was no chance of poking your gun. You had to swing the gun and quickly. A pack of wigeon appeared each side of me. I was so confused which to shoot at I ended up missing with two barrels. I put this right with the next pack taking a right and a left. The wigeon flight lasted about twenty minutes followed by some teal and mallard. The whole show lasted no more than half an hour. We had shot seven wigeon, three teal and two mallard. Lisa had picked everyone. The loch was long and about two hundred yards wide. There were hills climbing from both sides at the water's edge making it an ideal place for shelter for the ducks. Arriving in the dark not knowing the layout of the loch or the land, we were lucky we had built our hides in the perfect place.

At breakfast we decided to miss evening flight. We thought we would allow the geese to get back to their roost without disturbing them. With just one morning flight left, we were hoping it would finish in glory. That afternoon, relaxing and having a beer in the bar, we saw a character who we had seen in the bar on previous days. He had working clothes on and was sat studying the racing pages in the paper. We had noticed that most days there was a Council lorry loaded with salt in the car park at the rear of the hotel. We had remarked to each other that the roads could do with some of that salt. It didn't take long for Ian to start chatting with this fellow and it turned out that he was the lorry driver for the council. He told us that they only had one lorry and he was responsible for looking after the roads. Ian asked him why he wasn't out salting the roads. He replied, *"It's a waste of bloody time. The rain just washes it off again."* Then Ian asked him why he left the lorry's engine running all day while he was in the hotel. He replied, *"I have got to use the diesel up or the foreman will think I haven't been doing anything."* Ian said to him that our car had slipped on the ice and we nearly ended up in the ditch. *"I can believe that,"* he said, *"the roads here are treacherous."* Laughing, we went to our rooms and grabbed a couple of hours sleep before dinner.

After dinner the bar was starting to fill and there was an air of excitement. Tonight was the Ceilidh. The venue was a barn a mile down the road. Andy was encouraging us to go with them so we agreed. He then said, *"I had better tell you the rules. You are not allowed to have drink at the Ceilidh."* Ian's face dropped about a foot in sheer disappointment. Andy continued, *"Don't worry about it though Ian, if you haven't got a bottle in your pocket they won't let you in."* Ian laughed and immediately purchased two half bottles of whisky. What a wonderful time we had at the Ceilidh. There was a lady playing the squeeze box and two lads playing fiddles. Ian and

I didn't know the steps to the dances so we did a fair bit of improvisation. They made us really welcome. You would think they had known us for years. Alas, at one in the morning we staggered back to the hotel practising our Highland Dancing steps on the way.

Next morning we went back to the bushes. We didn't know what to expect. The wind had dropped the previous afternoon so there was a chance that the geese had gone back to their usual roost. We set up in position to wait. I was hoping the whitefronts would show again. As light started to break I heard the sound of geese. It seemed as though we would be in business again.

I could here them lifting from their roost one skein after another. The problem was they didn't seem to want to leave the loch. As day broke I could see them in the distance flying up and down the loch and all the time other skeins were lifting up to join them. The noise from the geese was incredible. I wish I had taken a tape recorder with me. Up and down the loch they went and my throat was getting sore from calling them. Whether it was my calling or sheer coincidence I don't know but the massive skein turned away from the loch and flew straight towards us. Andy certainly new what he was doing when he told us where to stand. This seems to be their favourite flight line. There were about a hundred birds in each formation with between twenty and thirty formations flying tightly together. The noise was deafening as they went over us. The geese at the front were about sixty yards up but as they were passing over I could see some skeins at the back which were considerably lower. We must have let a thousand geese go over before Ian fired a shot. I saw a goose fold and threw my own gun up taking a right and a left with both birds stone dead in the air. What a wonderful moment in my life. Since that day I have swung through geese with confidence rather than swing and hope. The whitefronts didn't show themselves and that was the last flight over. It wasn't long after that the Greenland whitefronts were put on the protected birds list. Consequently, I have never shot one. All I can claim is I got damned close.

That afternoon we went back to the fresh water loch. I looked through my binoculars down the loch and was thrilled to see two large rafts of wigeon at the other end. Will they come this way or will they go out at the other end? We didn't know but that's what it is all about. The hides we had used previously needed some attention and we settled in to wait. The wind was picking up by the minute. It is amazing how quickly the weather changes on Islay. By the time it was dusk the wind must have been seventy miles an hour. The wigeon came over me with the wind up their bums. They were so fast it was impossible to fire a shot. One second they were there and then they were gone. I have never been one for shooting where I think they might be. If I can't see them I don't shoot. Five packs of wigeon over me and not a shot fired.

The wind was howling but I thought I heard geese. I was straining my ears and they soon confirmed I was right. A quick change of cartridges to number one's and I was waiting. I could hear the geese for what seemed like a quarter of an hour and could tell from their calls they were getting closer. I was calling to them as they came on. Eventually they flew right over the top of me no more than ten yards high fighting against the wind. I put my gun down and absorbed a sight that most people will never see. The geese were working so hard to make any headway they never even noticed me. Ten minutes later it was pitch black and we were walking back to the car with the wind pushing us along. I hadn't fired a shot but what a wonderful way to finish the week.

The last night in the bar was special. Ian and I put the money we had left in a heap on the table. We took out enough for our petrol home and something to eat on the way. Thirty pounds was left. Ian gave it to Andy and said, *"Put that in your till and give drinks to everybody in the bar until the money has gone. When it has gone send us to bed."* Andy threw twenty pounds in with it and we all got pleasantly sloshed.

Next morning we were up early for the ferry. We had said our goodbyes the night before and had told them that we would slip out early without waking anyone. Surprisingly, when we went into the kitchen, Andy was placing two kippers under the grill for our breakfasts. As we were leaving he gave us both a present. It was a china haggis shaped as a bird with one leg longer than the other. Apparently these haggis live on the side of a hill and keep walking around it. Hence the short leg. The contents of this little gift was Beneagles whisky. There was a little rubber stopper in the bottom to empty it. I never emptied it. I kept it on my desk in my office and it stood there for years as a reminder. One day my wife decided to empty it. She gave the contents to her friend whilst I was at work.

The weather had changed again and the roads were like glass. We slid most of the way to the ferry but we had given ourselves plenty of time. When the ferry sailed into West Loch Tarbett I was surprised to see such a narrow stretch of water which the ferry had to navigate through. There were rocks sticking out of the water extremely close to the boat. I thought to myself, when we sailed out of here in the dark we were in the bar drinking whisky. We might have ended up with more water in our whisky than we normally take.

It was a long drive home which went without incident. We had lots of laughs relating to what had happened. I remember saying to Ian *"One day I am going to write a book about this."* We knew we had to go back the following year. In fact, I went back another five times.

I arrived home late at night. My wife was still up. As I walked in the room she turned her head and grunted *"you're back then."* It was a great shame she had stopped loving me. I often wonder if she ever did. I took great comfort though from the fact that my children loved me and so did my dog. The next day I was going through the post that had accumulated during the week. It had all been opened by my wife and the bills were there for me to attend to. *"A letter came with a compliment slip from a garage in Scotland,"* Irene said. *"It had two pound notes in it." "That's good,"* I said, *"Where are they?"* She replied, *"I have spent them!"*

CHAPTER 3

The Greg

It was during those boring months that I had the pleasure of meeting The Greg. The months between the close of the shooting season and the start of the rearing programme. I became involved with a group of people who started the Dunstable and District Clay Pigeon Club. We spent some of our leisure time in a pub just outside Dunstable. The pub had five acres of land adjacent to it which belonged to the brewery. The tenant landlord, who was affectionately known as Lord Effingham, for obvious reasons, became aware that we were looking for a suitable piece of ground to spend a Sunday morning shooting clay pigeons. With the idea in his mind that we would spend some money on his ale after the shooting, he suggested that we set up our traps on this field adjacent to the pub. The nearest house was a mile away so we decided to give it a try. Lord Effingham said, *"I will ring the effing brewery in the morning to see what they effing well say. They probably will effing well allow it as it is good for effing trade."*

News was good from the brewery so we set up three traps. 'Down the line', 'springing teal' and 'bolting rabbit'. Word soon passed around and on the first Sunday morning twenty people turned up to shoot. After four weeks we were up to forty people. Lord Effingham was delighted but insisted we stopped shooting at twelve noon because that was the opening time for the pub. We decided it was time to form a proper club and appoint officials, particularly a safety officer. Immediately after we had formed the club the luck of the Raw struck. Four miles away from the pub is a village. There was a man living in this village who was a Councillor. He was also a farmer and owned the fields that bordered part of the ground we were shooting on. He stated that he could hear the shooting in the village, which he didn't like, but apart from that, he deemed it to be dangerous that falling spent shot was possibly landing on his fields. We desperately tried to negotiate with this man but without success. He then wrote to the brewery complaining bitterly. The brewery took the sensible option and instructed us to remove the traps and cease the shooting. Their point was that when they applied for the annual renewal of the licence for the pub, they didn't want any enemies sitting on the bench.

One of the men who came to shoot was a character called The Greg. A man of tremendous enthusiasm and energy. Tall and stocky with red hair nearly down to his shoulders and a full red beard to match. He had pale blue eyes that turned pink after half a dozen gin and tonics. A man who oozed with confidence, with an air of arrogance and didn't seem to have much time for other people. I was lucky because he took to me. He was an exceptional character. It's over thirty years since I met him and I have never met anyone else to compare. Some people thought he was rude and selfish. I must admit he probably was, but only to the people he didn't have any time for. He became a member of our syndicate at Leverstock Green never missing a post-mortem in the pub afterwards.

The Greg. He turned out to be as mad as I am.

At that time I was sub-contracting and building thirty houses in a village twenty miles from Dunstable. The building site had previously been a farmer's field and the farmer lived next to the site in a large house with one hundred acres of ground. The farmer was getting on in years and after selling his field for a building site, he had retired. His son who lived at the other end of the village ran the farm. It was mainly poultry farming providing fertile eggs in their thousands. The hens and cockerels were in big sheds very tightly packed. The birds were worn out after only one season and were then sold to an Indian Restaurant for their speciality dishes. In my opinion the Indians put so much curry with everything you wouldn't know what you were eating.

The hundred acres consisted of fields that backed on to a massive forest. There was a track which was a public right of way through both the fields and the forest. It wasn't long before I was spending more time investigating than I was laying bricks. The forest held plenty of pheasants that wandered out into the fields during the day. A casual walk with my dog *Lisa* revealed to me the potential of this small piece of ground. I decided to approach the farmer's son to enquire about the possibilities of obtaining a lease for the shooting rights. *"Definitely not!"* he responded, *"My Father wouldn't allow me to lease it."*

Three weeks later the farmer's son came to see me on the building site. He asked me if I would carry out some building work for him at his house. Apparently, several builders had said they would do the work but nobody turned up to start the work when they said they would.

I went with him to his house to have a look. Once I had seen the proposed work I could see why nobody had turned up. He wanted a sun lounge building on the rear of his house. The bottom half was to be built in brick. Pigs had recently been foraging in the ground around the house, leaving the area where the sun lounge was to be constructed, like a bog. The proposed building required a foundation digging in the boggy ground. The foundation then needed to be concreted and the brick walls built up to mid way. The top half was to be timber frame and glazed. A typical farmer! The bricks were second hand, about fifty years old, soaking wet and dirty lying in a heap in the middle of the bog. I was quick to point out to him, that because of the conditions, he would find it difficult trying to find someone to carry out the work. I also told him if he did find someone willing to carry out the work they would charge him plenty to make it worth their while. Being a farmer, that really hurt him. His chin was dropping lower and lower. I was thinking to myself, if I keep this bad news up for much longer his chin will be in the mud. I then played my ace and made him a proposition. *"If you were to reconsider my request and allow me to shoot your Father's fields, I will carry out the work and I won't charge you."* Once he heard the words, I won't charge you, his face lit up as though someone had just told him the punch line of a hilarious joke. *"I can't give you a lease,"* he said, *"But you can take my word that you can shoot the ground as long as we own it, and we have no intentions of selling."* I felt like hugging him but decided against it. I built the sun lounge in the bog and he was delighted.

Two months later he came to see me again. There was a large chicken shed near his house and he wanted me to put a concrete road up to it. He had a contact for the readymix concrete but he wanted me to shutter the sides of the road and lay the concrete. The payment being offered was to shoot a one hundred and twenty acre pasture which was a mile up the road and belonged to his Aunt. I couldn't believe my luck. This pasture land backed onto the same forest. The following Sunday morning I walked the pasture which had several small copses and hedgerows. It was amazing at the amount of wildlife *Lisa* flushed out in half an hour. I was definitely going to be laying concrete next week.

It was mid summer so I decided to start feeding. Every day my tool kit included a bucket of wheat. At lunch time when the men were relaxing I was out feeding the fields outside the forest. The pheasants soon found the free meal and became regular feeders. I gradually fed further away from the forest until I had the pheasants coming the length of two fields for their dinner.

I took The Greg to my little shoot to show it to him. He was very impressed with the layout. I told him he would be invited to spend a day shooting with me when the season started and he looked pleased. He noticed there were a lot of pigeons flying into the forest to roost and suggested that we could have a shot at them before the season started. I agreed with him but I wanted the pigeon shooting to be well away from where I had been feeding the pheasants. I spent a couple of evenings that week just watching the pigeons to determine the flight lines so we could have some sport without disturbing the pheasants.

We didn't have the shooting rights in the forest so, one hour before sunset the following Saturday, we built our hides in the field ten yards out from the forest. Before long the pigeons started coming in to roost and we were in action shooting the pigeons out in front. After half an hour we had shot about thirty birds and they were spread about the field in front of us. I decided to collect them in. I thought if the birds flying in were to notice this battlefield, they would give it a wide berth. When I walked out I was amazed at what I found. When the pigeons had hit the ground their crops had burst open allowing the clover they had been eating to spill out. Incredibly, the clover had been tightly folded into their crops to achieve the maximum capacity.

I shouted at The Greg to come and have a look. Cupping my hands together I asked The Greg to empty the contents of a bird's crop into my palms. As the clover emptied from the crop it sprung out like elastic bands being released from tension. The contents of one crop filled both of my hands. If I hadn't seen it myself I would never have believed it.

Deciding we had shot enough for one day we tidied up the field and dismantled the hides. Before the season started we had two more evenings at the pigeons, both times shooting between thirty and forty birds. The pigeons were never wasted. Some were plucked and frozen ready for roasting and others had their breasts removed. I diced the breasts and mixed them with diced pork. They were then put into a suet pudding with chopped veg and a stock cube. Left to steam slowly, the meat was tender and the gravy, which had accumulated inside the suet pudding, was delicious. A recipe given to me by an old gamekeeper called Jack Collins.

One day while building a chimney stack on one of the houses ten Canada geese flew right over my head no more than twenty yards above me. I watched them fly over the farmhouse, on past the son's house and towards the end of the village where they dropped down and landed. My curiosity got the better of me. I abandoned the chimney and went looking in the direction the geese had flown. I found them in the pasture. Creeping along the hedgerow I lay in the bottom of the hedge watching them feeding. I lay there for an hour while the geese wandered over towards me chattering away to each other. At one point they were no more than fifteen yards away. I felt a weird sense of achievement being so close to these wild creatures without them knowing I was there. I suppose a man stalking would feel the same. I have never been deer stalking, although I am sure it is very skilful. It has never appealed to me to shoot at an animal that is standing still.

All the brickwork on the houses was now complete and I moved on to another site miles away from my little shoot. I could no longer feed every day so I set up some hoppers with enough food in them to last a week. Me and The Greg shot the little shoot many times that year. When I was getting ready for work in a morning I would think of my shoot and the pheasants wandering about. Maybe it wasn't such a good idea to have attracted the birds out into the open for everyone else to see, now that I am not there to look after them. Quite often I would say *"bugger the work."* I would put my dog and gun in the car and drive round to The Greg's house. The Greg had usually just returned home from working a night shift. At that time he was working as a tool maker. He would share his breakfast with me and then we were on our way to the shoot. It was usually about ten when we arrived at the farm and we would spend the morning slowly working the hedgerows and walking the fields. There were plenty of birds there. The feeding had certainly worked. Only selecting the difficult birds to shoot at, we kept the bag down to about a dozen. At lunch time we went to the village pub. The Greg always insisted on buying my lunch. We had a couple of pints, a meal and a game of dominoes playing fives and threes. We took our dominoes very seriously and I still do to this day. There is a lot of skill in the game and when I played The Greg, a game could last two hours. When we eventually finished the game we were off to the pasture for the afternoon. It was a brilliant little shoot because there was so much game on such a small area. Sometimes, we would both shoot at a pheasant at the same time. I would tease The Greg saying it was definitely me who hit the bird and not him. He would insist that he must have hit it because I was a crap shot. Occasionally he would ask, *"What size shot are you using?"* I would reply, sevens. He said he was using sixes and he would inspect the bird later. When we arrived back at his house he would carry out a biopsy on the poor pheasant, digging out the lead shot to determine who the killer was. Usually we had both hit it.

Taking *Lisa* home I bathed and fed her. After she had eaten she would lay in her basket in front of the fire with the most contented look on her face. She enjoyed the day as much as I did but she was useless at dominoes. I cleaned my gun, hung up the game, had a shower and ate my dinner. I was now ready to return to The Greg's house for a discussion on the days shooting. The Greg always missed the night shift after our days out. We would sit and play dominoes and set about a bottle of gin. As usual, after a few glasses of gin The Greg's eyes turned pink, like an albino. Every couple of hours The Greg's wife would come in with a plate of hot cheese on toast. We had wonderful evenings that usually went on until two in the morning. The Greg insisted that we had to finish the bottle before I went home. Of course, I didn't object too much.

We had been shooting the ground for two years when the luck of the Raw struck. I received a telephone call from a lady who was not very pleasant. It turned out that she was the Aunt of the farmer's son. She told me that someone had informed her that I had been shooting on her pasture and that I had no right to be there. She insisted that I must never go there again or she would report me to the police. I explained to her the agreement I had reached with her Nephew and that I had carried out work for him. The shooting was in a way of payment for the work. She was not interested in my explanation and told me he should not have made such an arrangement with me because he didn't own the ground. With that statement concluded, she put down the phone.

I went to see the farmer's son the following day to try and resolve the situation. I was sure that he would talk to her and I would be allowed to carry on shooting. I told him about the phone call from his Aunt. He smiled and replied, *"She is going senile."* I asked him if he would speak to her. *"She won't listen to me,"* he said. I then asked. *"What do I do about the shooting?"* he replied, *"If she said you can't shoot there, well that's it."* He was hosing down the road I had concreted while he was speaking to me. I felt like taking the hose pipe off him and inserting it in the rear end of his body. I didn't believe that he had ever discussed the shooting with his Aunt. I didn't blame her. Indeed, I respect other people's opinions about shooting and field sports. The relationship between me and the farmer's son was never the same again. He had a guilty conscience and he did his best to avoid me. The more I saw him, the more I felt like changing the structure of his face. If I had let The Greg loose at him he would have probably suffered the same fate as his chickens, ending up in some Indian curry. I have met many rogues in my life. Fortunately, I have also met some genuine people and The Greg was one of them. I shot the hundred acres for another season and then decided to stay away. Over the years The Greg has joined me on many wildfowling trips. He turned out to be as mad as I am.

CHAPTER 4

Tony Wallace

We shot at Leverstock Green every other Saturday. It was in the morning of one of the Saturdays that we didn't shoot when I rang The Greg. I asked him if he fancied shooting the pigeons coming in to roost at Blackwater Wood later in the day.

"I would like to but I am going partridge shooting this afternoon," he replied excitingly. *"Lucky you!"* I said, *"Where are you shooting?" "I am going to Letchworth, Tony Wallace invited me."* I asked him, *"Who is Tony Wallace?" "He is a fireman. I'm surprised you haven't heard of him. Come along with me and I will introduce you to him."* I thanked him for his offer but explained that I didn't like to tag along uninvited. *"What a load of rubbish!"* shouted The Greg, laughing, *"Tony won't mind at all. I will pick you up at eleven."* I hadn't had a shot at a partridge since my apprenticeship days and the prospect really whetted my appetite. *"Are you sure?"* I said. *"Of course I am, you worry too much. I will be at your house at eleven."*

I was ready in plenty of time and while I was eating some early lunch I was talking to my dog *Lisa*. She had never seen a partridge and I was telling her all about them. *Lisa* was listening to me intently. She probably didn't know exactly what I was going on about but she could sense that I was excited. She knew that what excited me also excited her. My wife remarked. *"You must be bloody stupid talking to the dog like that, she doesn't understand."* I didn't like to tell her that *Lisa* understood me far more than she ever did.

The Greg arrived at twelve, as boisterous as ever. He had a new spaniel with him called Winston. He was telling me someone he knew had owned Winston for two years and kept him down in a cellar. The poor dog had hardly seen the light of day. The Greg heard that they were looking for a new home for the dog so he took him. Winston was the friendliest dog you would ever wish to meet. Unfortunately, he had no interest whatsoever in hunting. I think he must have misplaced his bum at some time because he spent the whole day sniffing the other dog's bums, as if he was trying to find the one he had lost.

The Greg had a Ford Escort car. God knows what was under the bonnet but the bloody thing went like a rocket. The Greg was driving as usual, talking and waving his hands around with the accelerator hard down on the floor. He frightened me to death without even realising it. He wasn't showing off. That was the way The Greg always drove. Every now and then he would overtake some innocent driver who was stupid enough to be driving within the speed limit. They would get a blast of the horn and a mouthful of abuse, which was just thrown into the middle of the conversation we were having. If I had asked him why he had shouted at the driver of the car five minutes ago, he would have said, *"What car? I don't remember."* It was just the way of The Greg.

It's about twenty-five miles to Letchworth from Dunstable and I was pleased to arrive there in one piece. I sat in the passenger seat, in the crash position, always expecting the worst to happen at the next bend. By the time we arrived I was a bag of nerves with white knuckles from hanging on to the dashboard for dear life.

We drove onto a housing estate and stopped outside a gate where a man was standing rolling a cigarette. He had a shrunken hat on, that had obviously been with him for a number of years. It had taken the shape of his head. A Red Setter dog sat next to him. Glancing up momentarily he grinned at The Greg, then eyes back down to the roll up.

The Greg leapt out of the car and walked towards the man. As he slammed the car door the bloody car started to roll backwards. I grabbed the hand brake and pulled on it. It brought the car to a halt as the brake lever reached the top of the ratchet. The Greg turned around and roared with laughter. Getting out of the car I walked over to them. The man carried on meticulously rolling his cigarette cone shaped. There can't have been more than six strands of tobacco in it. The Greg, still laughing said, *"Tony, this is Vince Raw, a friend of mine. I have brought him along to join us."* I extended my arm to shake Tony's hand. I don't think he noticed it. He was cautiously lighting his roll up, which consisted of eighty percent paper. After he had successfully negotiated the lighting procedure without setting fire to his face, he turned around and walked up the garden path towards his house. *"Come and have a cup of tea and meet Pat,"* he muttered. We followed him into the kitchen and sat down. I didn't know what to make of Tony. Was he purposely trying to be rude? Maybe he never noticed my gesture of friendship. Pat came into the kitchen with a broad smile on her face.

Her hair was dark, quite long and in tight curls. It reminded me of a portrait I had once seen of 'The Laughing Cavalier'. *"Hello Greg, how are you?"* she enquired laughingly, *"Raring to go,"* The Greg replied, *"I have brought my friend Vince with me."* I didn't know whether to hold out my hand or not, so I just said hello. *"Hello Vince, how many sugars in your tea?"* I answered, *"No sugar for me thanks, I'm sweet enough."* *"Like hell you are,"* roared The Greg.

Tony rolling a cigarette.

By this time Tony was busy selecting another suitable six strands of tobacco for another roll up. Pat made the tea and we had a mug full each. The Greg and Tony were in conversation about muzzle loading shotguns. They spoke of the new club they had joined where people were shooting clay pigeons with muzzle loaders and flint locks. I listened to them with interest, although, I must admit, I couldn't wait to get at the partridge. The kettle went on again and we had another pot of tea. Eventually, after what seemed to be forever but was probably half an hour, Tony said it was time we were going. We got up from the table to follow Tony out. He arrived at the door opening and stopped to roll another cigarette. We stood behind him and waited until he had performed this function and watched him light it. When he lit it, the bloody thing burnt down to half its length with the first draw. I remember thinking, that's not going to last long, he will probably stop at the gate to roll another.

Tony put the Red Setter into his jeep and we followed him to the farm where we were to shoot. The Red Setter's name was Lucky. He was a beautiful looking dog. One of the biggest Red Setters I had ever seen. Five minutes later we arrived at the farm. I was pleasantly surprised to find that there was nobody else there. I expected a few more people to be waiting for us. The farm was quite small and consisted of about ten large fields. Tony insisted that we should meet the farmer and took us to the house. The farmer had retired and leased the fields to others. Because of health problems he was not allowed to drive. Tony was telling us that in the fire service they work two night shifts, two day shifts and then have four days off. When he wasn't working he would often drive the farmer around. The farmer had a wonderful collection of old clocks and watches. Tony sometimes drove him hundreds of miles just to go and see an old watch.

After another cup of tea we went back to the car for the guns and dogs. I was ready in thirty seconds. Tony rolled a cigarette and then we wandered out of the farmyard towards the fields. The fields were mainly barley stubble although a couple of them had been ploughed. There were hedgerows between the fields that had been trimmed down to about five feet. It reminded me of the fields we used to shoot when I was an apprentice. I really enjoy shooting in small parties. You may well end up with a larger bag when there are plenty of guns and beaters but it is more enjoyable shooting with just a couple of friends.

Tony took us along a hedge and positioned me about twenty yards from a gate. He took The Greg about a hundred yards further up the hedge. He then went along the hedge which led on to a track about a quarter of a mile away. I could see him walking up the track and cutting across so he was heading back towards us from the other end of this huge field. I was thinking, he will never be able to cover this field on his own, it is far too big.

I could see him in the centre of the field but he was stationary. I realised he must have been rolling another cigarette. Before long, he set off towards us working his dog. What a wonderful sight watching that Red Setter work. Without rushing or tearing about, the dog was quartering, covering the whole field. Always under complete control. *Lisa* had sat herself in the hedgerow so she could see up the field. Almost immediately her tail started to wag. I stood there ready. A hare casually ran down the field and through the gate. It was closely followed by two more. Minutes later more hares. I counted fourteen hares that went through the gate from the field. Tony was halfway down the field when a covey of partridge took to the air. They came straight down the field and swung over The Greg. The Greg opened fire with two barrels. Two partridge fell with the first barrel and nothing with the second. A few moments later another covey came towards me. They were no more than eight feet off the ground. I couldn't shoot out in front because of Tony and Lucky. I didn't want to shoot low sideways or behind because I didn't know the layout of the surrounding land. I started to wave my arm to try and put them up higher. Most of them just screamed over me but two at the back of the covey swung up nearly vertically, offering a safe chance. I managed to take one of them with my second barrel. Tony and Lucky were getting close so I broke my gun and removed the cartridges. As I took them out another large covey sprung up and swung right across me settling down three fields away. I sent *Lisa* out to pick the partridge I had shot which she did without any fuss. The Greg shouted of me to help him pick up. He had picked one but he couldn't find the other. The Greg was hunting through the stubble and Winston was sat admiring him. I sent *Lisa* over to him and it wasn't long before she was heading back to me with the partridge. She had company though. Winston was running in harmony with her with his nose stuck firmly up her bum. Tony came through the gate with a grin on his face. He leant against the gate and rolled a cigarette. Lucky sat next to him to prevent Winston examining his rear end. Tony looked up at me and said, *"You never had a shot at the hares Vince."* I explained that I didn't really like to shoot hares. *"You are the same as me"* he said, *"I haven't shot a hare for years. I have a rule here, whoever shoots the hare can carry it."* He took us across a road to some more stubble fields. Lining us out again before he walked off with Lucky. Ten minutes later he was there at the top of the field coming towards us. This field had its share of hares but not quite as many as the first field. A small covey of partridges flew over The Greg, at what seemed like eighty miles an hour. The Greg took one with his second barrel. Almost immediately another small covey was up and flying away from us. Tony had a right and left at a good forty yards. I watched Lucky retrieve them. He picked up one, tossed it to the back of his mouth and then picked up the other. He delivered them both to Tony with such gentleness, it was a delight to watch.

We stood talking for a while and had a cigarette. I didn't usually smoke during the day but I enjoyed one in circumstances like that. Lucky growled at Winston who had made another determined attempt to sniff his bum. Tony took us to the field where the large covey had flown to earlier. On the way to the field I offered to do the walking with *Lisa* so Tony could have a stand but he wouldn't hear of it. Me and The Greg lined out behind the hedge at the bottom. Tony and Lucky walked the field. They were about a third of the way down the field when the covey lifted. Once again they swung out to the side, not giving a chance. I saw them fly across the road where we had just been. They dropped down onto a ploughed field. There were no more partridges in the field we were working but there were several hares. I noticed that The Greg was refraining from shooting the hares. He obviously didn't relish the idea of carrying them.

Tony decided that we would walk the ploughed field in a line. He said the partridge would probably sit tight in the plough giving us a chance to get near them. We were halfway across the field when the luck of the Raw struck. I lost my footing in the plough and fell onto my knees. At the same time the bloody covey leapt up in front of me. Once again they flew to the side but this time they had made a bad choice. Tony took another right and left and The Greg killed one with his second barrel. I was down on my knees cursing my luck. I looked at *Lisa*. I am sure she had a grin on her face. Tony decided that we had shot enough partridges for one day so we headed back to the vehicles. Lucky was caught off his guard as he was about to jump into the jeep. Winston was straight in with his nose. Lucky whipped round and nipped Winston's ear. Winston didn't seem to mind, he had checked out Lucky's bum and that was very important to him.

Going over to Tony I thanked him for a great afternoon. *"It's not over yet!"* he replied, *"Come back and see Pat."* We went back to Tony's house. Pat was just taking some home baked bread out of the oven. It smelt wonderful. The Table was set with plates and knives. The bread was placed on the table, closely followed with a pack of butter, block of cheese and mugs of hot tea. I could get used to this very quickly, I thought. No wonder The Greg turned down the pigeon shooting.

Pat's kitchen, where we enjoyed the home made bread.

We were talking about all aspects of shooting while we were stuffing our faces. I mentioned to Tony about my love of duck shooting. He asked me, *"Have you ever shot ducks coming into a pond vertically?"* I told him I didn't think I had. He looked at his watch and said, *"We have just got time, follow me."* We were in the vehicles and off again. Driving out of the town and pulling off the road outside an old building that looked like a village hall. Walking around the back of the building and fifty yards into a wood we came to a small pond. There were trees growing out of the pond and all the way around it. I looked up and the tree canopy almost completely enclosed the pond. It was getting dark now and Tony put me in behind a bush twenty-five yards away from the pond. *"You will have to be quick,"* he said, *"they drop like stones."* Ten minutes later four mallard came crashing in through the canopy like bullets. I fired from pure reaction and I shot my first right and left at mallard. A few minutes later The Greg opened up and I heard a splash into the water. I looked to where Tony was standing. He still had his gun in its sleeve strapped across his back. He had a big grin on his face as he was rolling a cigarette. After lighting his cigarette he said, *"That will do for today. Let's go back and see Pat."*

We went back and finished off the bread which was immediately replaced by another hot loaf. We brought the dogs in the kitchen and Tony produced a bottle of whisky. The Greg tried to claim a right and a left at the first covey of partridges. I saw the two birds fall from his first barrel so he was overruled. He just laughed and poured himself a whisky.

Tony was telling me that he had thousands of acres to shoot on. Letchworth was the first Garden City and apparently the Council own the land and all the farms are leased. Tony wrote to the Council offering to carry out vermin control. No doubt the fact that he worked for the Council as a leading Fireman, based in Letchworth, had some bearing on their decision to allow him a huge part of the land to shoot on. He was telling me about the amount of pigeons that he shot over decoys and coming in to roost. He was also shooting ducks on barley stubble. I listened with great interest. When we were leaving he took my telephone number and said he would ring me one day to have a go at the pigeons. I thanked him and Pat and ventured outside. The whisky had given me the opportunity to take a good anaesthetic before my journey back home in The Greg's racing car.

This happened thirty years ago and was the first of numerous days I have spent with Tony. He, without any doubt, is the most unselfish person I have ever been out shooting with, always insisting that I should be put in the best position. He is a good shot and has great respect for his quarry taking only sporting shots. The right and left mallard I shot turned out to be a duck and a drake which I had mounted. They are still with me today.

Tony and Pat became good friends and still are. They live in Scotland just fifteen miles from me. We both live close to the foreshore at Wigtown Bay but on opposite sides. Ironically, we spend far more time watching the foreshore and counting the geese than we do shooting it. We still occasionally shoot together but we enjoy more time these days working our dogs together on other people's shoots. Wigtown Bay has been declared a Local Nature Reserve and shooting is by a permit system. The geese have a safe roosting area where no shooting is allowed and there are some restrictions on the hours for shooting. I am a member of a local wildfowling club and we have representatives on the Wigtown Bay Local Nature Reserve Management Committee to put the view of the wildfowler forward.

Tony has continued to roll his cigarettes cone shaped. Pat still has the same hair style and it really suits her. I'm sure she will forgive me for my earlier remarks about the cavalier.

CHAPTER 5

First trips to the Ouse Washes

After desperately looking for months we finally found a place to start the clay pigeon club again. It was in an old quarry where chalk had been extracted to make lime. The white faced walls of the quarry gave the ideal background for clay shooting. The drawback was the wind which seemed to rebound from the quarry walls and swirl around. You could never be sure how the clays would react when the wind caught them. Sometimes they would lift up, as is often the case at most clay shoots. The next clay you called for could well do the total opposite. Local knowledge helped a bit, but not always. I was trying to obtain a badge for shooting a straight fifty at, 'down the line.' On two separate occasions the fiftieth clay dipped as I pulled the trigger. Well, that's my excuse anyway.

The membership of the club had grown rapidly which meant there was a chance to meet new faces and listen to new ideas. One Sunday morning a chap we called Hammer was at the clay shoot. He was the chairman of the Muzzle Loaders Club and we called him Hammer because of the noise he made at the monthly meetings. He had a wooden gavel which he was constantly banging on the table as he was shouting for order. Some chance with The Greg there and the meetings being held in a pub. He has been called Hammer for so long I have forgotten what his real name is. A serious sort of person with long thick sideburns. Being quite knowledgeable when it came to guns he used to brown coat the Damascus barrels, using the rusting process, for the club members.

Hammer was telling us about a place called the Ouse Washes. In my ignorance I had never heard of them. According to what he had been told there were thousands of wigeon there. When people start talking like that it makes the hairs on the back of my neck stand up. Apparently he was going to make some enquiries about shooting there. He was asking if anybody would be interested in going with him. Interested! The nerves in my guts started to take over and I had to make an emergency exit to the nearest loo. The Greg managed to shut Hammer up before the other members heard him because we don't like big shooting parties. There was me and The Greg, Hammer and a fellow called Stan, who had a wonderful collection of guns. Stan was a very meticulous sort of person.

Everything he did had to be done correctly and he would not be rushed. He was quite recognisable because he nearly always had a dew drop hanging off the end of his nose. We asked Hammer to try and obtain details from his friend about booking some shooting. Hammer said he would do that and he would inform us of the outcome the following week.

The week seemed to take a month to pass and I was dreaming of wigeon. Lying in bed wondering what news Hammer would bring with him on Sunday morning. I don't know why but I seem to be totally addicted to duck shooting. Most people dream of owning a Rolls Royce. I dream of owning my own duck pond.

Hammer turned up on the Sunday morning and I was anxious to hear what he had to say. His friend had been telling him that there were several washes. Some were owned by the Wetland Wildlife Trust and were used as a reserve. Some were owned by the Fenland Wildfowlers Club and private individuals while others were auctioned each year to farmers for the grazing. The farmers would then let the shooting rights. Hammer's friend had been to a wash called Willow Wash obtaining a permit from a gun shop in Wisbech for morning flight. He had said there were a lot of wigeon flighting over the wash although they were too high to shoot at.

We all agreed that we would give it a try. Hammer said he would write to the gun shop and obtain the permits. Deciding that it was a long way to go for just one flight we were going to book the wash for the day, which would give us evening flight as well.

I went to the library the next day to try and find some information on The Ouse Washes. I read with interest. The Ouse Washes is a strip of land situated between two rivers which eventually terminate at The Wash and it is purposely flooded. It is three quarters of a mile wide and over twenty miles long. Apparently, the first river was cut in the sixteen hundreds and was partly funded by The Duke of Bedford. Hence the name, the Old Bedford River. The intention was to improve summer grazing for cattle. More permanent drainage was required which led to the excavation of the New Bedford River, which is also known as the Hundred foot River, that being the distance between the tops of the embankments either side.

In the winter months from January onwards the washes are purposely flooded. The area of ground that drains into these rivers is huge and because the fall to The Wash is so shallow, plus the fact that the tide backs the water up the rivers, the water cannot escape fast enough. Therefore, the washes are allowed to be flooded. This is to prevent accidental flooding to the rest of the Fens

A few days later Hammer was on the phone. He had received a reply from the gun shop and he suggested the four of us had a meeting to discuss tactics. We arranged to meet in a pub the next night. The information Hammer had received told us that the access to Willow Wash was at the bridge over the New Bedford River at Mepal. There is a pub next to the river adjacent to the bridge called The Three Pickerels. It was suggested that the vehicle should be parked in the car park of the pub. We should then venture on foot over the bridge and through a gate on the opposite side of the road. Willow Wash was about one and a half miles down a track and situated between the two rivers behind a small wood. To enable us to find the wash in the dark it was noted that there was an unused house boat moored next to the wash.

Hammer had obtained four permits for the Saturday. The debate started about whose vehicle we were going in. How long would it take etc. Hammer said that he would like to travel Friday night to make sure he would have plenty of time to find the wash in the dark. The Greg liked the idea. He suggested that we could have a few beers in The Three Pickerels, then wander down to Willow Wash and sleep in the unused house boat. Stan had other arrangements for the Friday night and stated that he would have to travel early on the Saturday morning. I have been to the pub with The Greg on many occasions just to have a few beers and often regretted it the next day. I decided not to let the pub ruin my duck shooting and offered to travel with Stan. That was the arrangements sorted. Hammer and The Greg were going Friday night and me and Stan would see them there on the Saturday morning.

Stan arrived at my house at quarter past three on Saturday morning as arranged. I had been ready for an hour and my nervous stomach had forced me to visit the loo four times while I was waiting. I get so excited at times like this I think it would pay me to wear some incontinent pants. We travelled in Stan's car. I laid a blanket down on the floor of the car for my dog *Lisa* and she lay under my legs with her head on my foot. She realised something was happening and was as excited as me. Stan drove the car and I noticed the usual dew drop in place. He told me calmly that he had never been duck shooting before and I was amazed that he didn't show any signs of excitement. I had been over twenty times and the anticipation of duck flighting was still affecting the butterflies in my stomach.

Duck shooting was hard to come by where we lived. Of course there were ponds and reservoirs but it was virtually impossible to obtain the shooting rights. I often travelled to the Nene Estuary during the week, when I should really have been at work. At ten-thirty in the morning I would put the gun and my hide in the car and head off to Wisbech with *Lisa* sat beside me. Collecting a permit I would drive to the Nene Estuary, parking next to the lighthouse where the famous Peter Scott had lived. Usually arriving about three, with hide, gun and bag secured to my back, I would set off to the foreshore and out onto the mud with *Lisa* at my heel. I realised after the first couple of times I had been, the chances of shooting duck on evening flight were pretty slim. Yet the anticipation that I might be lucky and the pure peace just being there listening to the wading birds was enough to make me return time after time. On several occasions ducks had flighted off at dusk but always too far away to have a shot.

There was one time I went that will remain in my head for as long as I live. I don't know exactly how many times I had been before without success but it must have been in double figures. This day was going just the same as the rest. Me and *Lisa* sat behind our hide, which I used to cover with mud for camouflage, listening to the waders and just enjoying the moment. It was getting dark and the birds' chorus had gone quiet when I just made out the shape of mallard straight over me. They looked high but I decided that they should be in range if I could see them so I swung the gun through one of them and fired a shot. I thought I saw the bird drop down lower than the rest of them and then I lost it in the dark. Listening intently I thought I heard a bird hit the mud a long way behind me. I looked at *Lisa*. She had definitely heard something and was waiting for instructions. *"Get on,"* I said, and she was off. I heard her crossing creeks and then I could hear nothing.

After five minutes it was pitch black and I was starting to be concerned for the dogs safety. Deciding to whistle her in, I had just put the whistle to my mouth when she came from behind me with a beautiful drake mallard in her mouth. I cannot explain the emotion I felt. I grabbed hold of *Lisa* and hugged her. What a wonderful dog she was. While I was hugging and kissing her, my face got covered in mud from her but I didn't care. I felt completely overwhelmed. We stopped at Wisbech on the way home for our supper. I bought two portions of fish and chips. *Lisa* sat on the passenger seat of the car and we shared the supper. I was so pleased with her I just couldn't stop stroking her and telling her what a good girl she was. She took full advantage of the situation and lay on the seat with her head on my knee all the way home. It was my first mallard off The Wash. I wouldn't like to add up how much it had actually cost. It didn't matter. In the circumstances it was priceless.

I have read stories where people shoot seventy wigeon on one flight. It has never happened to me, nor would I want it to. I have always had to work hard to shoot wildfowl and I am sure it makes you appreciate the odd success. It has something to do with the hunting instinct that has been passed down to some of us from many years ago, when it was a man's duty to hunt and provide a meal for the family. It's a good job my family doesn't rely on me to shoot their food. They certainly wouldn't be overweight.

We found The Three Pickerels car park without too much trouble and parked next to The Greg's car. It was still one and a half hours to day break. After getting out of Stan's car I looked in The Greg's car. The Greg and Hammer were in there fast asleep. You could here the snores from The Greg at the other side of the car park. I tapped on the driver's side window and woke them up. The Greg wound down his window and shouted, *"I wouldn't go sailing in that bloody house boat if I was you. There's no effing bottom in it."* He then swung open his door and I noticed that he was sitting in his long johns. He carried on shouting. *"I jumped on to the bloody boat to see what it was like and I dropped straight into four bloody feet of freezing cold water."* I started to laugh and Stan joined me. Eventually I stopped laughing and asked if there was any water on the wash. *"I don't know,"* shouted The Greg, *"As soon as I had been half drowned I came back to the car. My waders are full up with water, my trousers are soaking wet, I have had the heater on in the car for the last three hours and my long johns have dried on me."* I told him not to worry. I had spare trousers with me and Stan had a spare pair of Wellington boots. I noticed his eyes were pink and asked. *"Have you been on the gin Greg?"* He had calmed down a bit and replied quietly, *"Just a few to help me sleep."* I asked him if he always drank gin before swimming. His reply was something like, *"You sarcastic bastard!"* I decided not to take the urine for a while. Well, at least not for ten minutes. I asked him what it was like in The Three Pickerels. *"Nearly as bloody cold as it was in that water!"* he said.

Getting ready for our walk we were listening to The Greg complaining bitterly that the Wellington boots Stan had lent him must belong to Stan's wife. He said the bloody things were four sizes too small. His thick socks were still wet and his feet wouldn't go in the boots with them on. I had a thin pair of socks in my bag and I offered to rent them to him. *"Give them to me you tight fisted sod,"* he said and started laughing. That's more like it I thought. We are back to normal. We were ready to go but we had to wait for Stan. He had brought a beautiful English ten bore side by side and was carefully removing it from its leather case and placing it in a sleeve. Then the cartridges had to be selected. Number fours in one pocket, sixes in another and a couple of ones in a front pocket in case we saw any geese. I am all for being well prepared but this process took the best part of twenty minutes.

We eventually walked through the gate to head up the track to the wash. *"Be careful!"* said The Greg, *"There is a muddy puddle about two feet deep just inside the gate. If we go to the right we can go round it."* The rest of the track wasn't too bad to walk on, apart from being a bit slippery. It was on the top of the embankment running parallel with the New Bedford River.

I was wondering if there would be any water on the wash. According to the information I had read, the washes were flooded between January and March. It was now just at the beginning of December. I will find out soon enough I thought, and carried on up the track following The Greg who was jokingly complaining that the socks I had lent him were too thin.

Arriving at the wood in front of Willow Wash, I picked up the house boat in my torch light. It wasn't in the river. It was in a deep ditch in front of the wood. Walking over a small bridge that crossed the ditch, we were now on Willow Wash which was not flooded. We were walking through long grass and rushes. I shone the torch panning the wash. There were two ponds, one at each side about a hundred yards apart. We decided the best approach would be to have two guns on each pond. Hammer and The Greg went to the furthest pond and me and Stan to the other.

There were hides already constructed around the ponds and we settled in to them. Just in time I thought, I could see the day was starting to break. Stan was about twenty-five yards to my right. I could just about make him out, moving about cautiously, getting himself ready. God knows what he would be like in an emergency. After about ten minutes six mallard flew over Stan about fifteen yards high. If he hadn't been there I would have fired at them but I thought I would leave them for him. On they flew and not a sound from Stan's mighty weapon. A few moments later four shots rang out from the other pond. The day was breaking fast and whether the shooting is good or not it is a wonderful experience just being there to witness it. I could see Stan clearly now. He was sat there with his head dead still. He never looked around once to see if any ducks were coming. I saw a lone wigeon heading towards Stan from behind. It was about thirty yards up. There was little chance that it was coming into the pond as it was flying very fast, obviously heading to somewhere better. I knew Stan wouldn't see it, so I shot it when it was twenty yards behind him. It was dead but the speed it was travelling gave it enough momentum to crash into Stan as it came down. Stan leapt up in fright as though he had just woken up.

That was the flight over and it was daylight. I saw a harrier fly over the wood and then swoop low hunting over the wash. The sun was starting to show indicating it was going to be a sunny day. Not the best of weather for duck flighting! We gathered back into a group and stood at the edge of the wood. The Greg had shot a cock wigeon, mine was a hen. While we were talking, we saw a massive pack of wigeon fly along the wash, parallel with and between the rivers, about four gunshots high. They were soon followed by another large pack at the same height. We decided to stand in the wood and see if there were any birds flying in range. In the next hour we saw literally thousands of wigeon all on the same flight line and all at the same height.

The Greg said he was hungry and suggested we should go back and have something to eat. We walked back across the little bridge over the ditch. Now we could have a look at the house boat where The Greg had come to grief. It was wedged in the ditch and looked as though it had been there for years. I surmised that at some time in the past someone probably used it to shoot out of when the washes were flooded. I looked over the gunwales. The floor had virtually gone. I am sure if The Greg hadn't swilled so much gin in The Three Pickerels he would have taken more time to investigate the boat before jumping into it.

Arriving back at the gate I could see the great puddle of mud The Greg had mentioned earlier. As we walked round it I couldn't help thinking what a stupid place to put a gate. I realised later that the quagmire was caused by the cattle. Before the washes were flooded the cattle were brought down to the gate for collection.

Walking around, waiting for the transporting lorries, they created this hole. We walked across the road into the car park. Stan set about cleaning his gun and placing it back in the leather case. After about fifteen minutes he was still buggering about when The Greg roared at him, *"For Christ's sake Stan, will you hurry up, I'm bloody starving and I we want to find a café. You will be using the bloody gun again in a few hours time. The speed you're going, it will be time to take it out before you have put it away."* Stan obviously didn't know The Greg very well because he jumped up in surprise and cracked the back of his head on the open lid of the boot. The Greg roared at him again, *"That's the fastest you have moved all day and your bloody dew drop has fallen off."*

"Your bloody dew drop has fallen off!"

When I had stopped laughing, I informed The Greg that it was the second time the dew drop had fallen off today. The first time was when I dive bombed Stan with a wigeon.

After driving a few miles we found a café where we had a big fried breakfast. Lorry drivers kept coming in and from their conversation it was obvious that the man behind the counter was called Joe. I gave the café the nickname of Greasy Joe's and we used it on many occasions later.

While eating I asked Stan if he had seen the mallard fly over him at first light. *"Yes, I saw them,"* he said. A stupid question I know, but I asked him why he didn't have a shot at them. He replied. *"I wasn't quite ready. I hadn't put the cartridges in."* I found it unbelievable, that after all the planning and preparation how anyone can forget to put the cartridges in. Over the years I have seen Stan do just that, on many occasions.

Returning to the car with a sausage sandwich for *Lisa*, we drove to Chatteris to kill some time. What a charming little place it was. I was thinking it would be a handy place to stay if we came to shoot Willow Wash for more than one day. We drove back to Mepal and followed The Greg into The Three Pickerels for a pint. It was colder in the pub than it was outside. The walls were painted with a purple coloured emulsion, which didn't make it feel any warmer. The place was empty apart for the man behind the bar reading a paper. He looked up with a grin on his face, *"Hello, my wildflowers. How are you today?"* The Greg immediately went on the attack and said, *"Albert, you didn't tell me the house boat was a wreck and full of bloody water."* I remember thinking, it didn't take The Greg long to find out the landlord's name. Albert replied with a huge grin on his face, *"You didn't ask me!"* The Greg looked at him and shouted, *"I told you I was going to sleep in the bloody thing, didn't I?"* Albert looked up from his paper and said. *"I know you said you were going to sleep in it but you didn't ask me if there was any water in it. I know there is a big hole in the bottom of it and the water could have drained out."* I found this remark highly amusing and burst into laughter. Albert still had a big grin on his face and it wasn't long before The Greg was laughing as well. I think if The Greg could have got hold of Albert in the early hours, he would have throttled him. The Greg always mellowed with alcohol and it was all soon forgotten.

Albert was a stout man, probably in his middle sixties. Over the years that we shot The Ouse Washes I got to know him quite well. He had a good sense of humour and would play tricks on you at every opportunity. People would come into the pub and state, *"It's cold in here Albert!"* He had a classic answer and I must have heard him say it fifty times. *"If you think it's cold over there. You wouldn't like to be at this side of the bar, I am standing over the cellar"*.

We were chatting to Albert and he was showing us tricks with cards and matches. I was more interested in learning something about the shooting on the washes. He was very vague on this subject and didn't seem to want to tell us too much. I asked him if trade was good. He told me he often had a party of six wildflowers shooting on the washes for a week and they helped his turnover. I asked him if the shooters stayed in his pub. *"Oh no. They stay in a shed about a mile and a quarter past the house boat and shoot Pontoon Wash."* The mention of the house boat brought another big grin to his face. I asked him who owned Pontoon Wash. It turned out to be the same gun shop that owned Willow Wash.

I had to go and have a look at the shed and Pontoon Wash. It was now half past one. I asked the boys if they wanted to come with me to have a look. We could shoot the evening flight on Willow Wash on the way back. The Greg was in full flow now and wasn't keen to leave the pub until closing time at half past two. Knowing The Greg it would be more like three before we got him out. Hammer wasn't much of a drinker and was still only half way down the half pint he had asked for. Stan was sat at a table looking absolutely frozen. The dew drop on the end of his nose was about to crystallise. The Greg reluctantly bowed to the majority vote and we left the pub. *"Don't forget to return,"* Albert laughingly retorted, *"Wildflowers are always welcome in here,"* The Greg muttered, *"I bet bloody Eskimos are as well."*

We walked back up the muddy track against a stiffening breeze. I could see the wood in front of Willow Wash in the distance but it never seemed to get any closer. Eventually we were alongside the house boat that The Greg loved so much. Leaving our guns and bags hidden in the wood, we carried on to find the wash with a shed. It was a long way and the track deteriorated. The wind was really picking up forcing us to lean into it. The Greg was moaning that the pub may have been cold but at least it wasn't windy. He then turned round and spoke to Stan. *"It will keep the end of your nose dry, if nothing else."* I think Stan was getting a bit fed up with this constant reference to his nose from his remark of *"clever bastard!"*

It was just after three when we arrived at Pontoon Wash. The ditch, which the house boat was in continued parallel with the track as far as you could see. There was a small bridge over the ditch to gain access onto the wash. The shed, as Albert called it, turned out to be a log cabin built on ten foot timber stilts with steps up to a balcony. I could now see how the wash had derived its name. The cabin was built as a pontoon. There was no sign of life in the cabin and curiosity got the better of me. Climbing up the steps on to the balcony I looked through the window. I tried the door and it opened so I went in. There were six bunks set out in three lots of two high, a sink, Calor Gas cooker and table and chairs. The lights were small twelve volt bulbs which were powered from a battery. The battery was charged from a windmill which was crudely fixed onto a piece of wood which was nailed to the side of the cabin. The mattresses on the bunks were muddy but that wouldn't matter if you had a sleeping bag. I went back out on to the balcony that faced the wash. This wash was far bigger than Willow Wash and several ponds had been excavated. I could see three quarters of a mile across to the Old Bedford River and that was the extent of Pontoon Wash. What a find! It was absolutely wonderful. What a place to lose yourself for a few days. I was definitely going to go back there.

We hurried back to Willow Wash with the wind behind us. Everybody was happy with the positions they had taken in the morning so we took the same hides. I was watching Stan. It was nearly dark by the time he had sorted himself out and even then you couldn't be sure he had any cartridges in his gun. A pair of mallard were crossing out in front of me. I could have shot at them but I left them for Stan. They flew right across in front of him and he never saw them. I decided then I wouldn't leave the next ones. Unfortunately, no more came our way. There were five shots from the other pond and then it was dark. I heard the call I have heard many times from The Greg. *"Fetch your dog!"* I went across with *Lisa*. Hammer had shot two wigeon but they couldn't find them. Hammer pointed to where the birds had dropped and I sent *Lisa* on. She was straight back with a cock wigeon. I sent her again. She started to work away from the place Hammer had said they had fallen. "Call her back," shouted Hammer, *"It is definitely where I showed you. I marked it down."* I said, *"Just let her work. She knows what she is doing." Lisa* vanished into the darkness and I could see the frustration on Hammer's face. A couple of minutes later she was back with a hen wigeon, which I had to kill. Without a thank you or a pat for the dog, Hammer quickly put both ducks into his bag and that's were they stayed. I thought he might have given one to Stan but that was the last thing on his mind. I think he had a picture in his mind of these two wigeon sitting on his dinner plate.

By the time we had walked back The Three Pickerels was open again. We had another hour with Albert and we were on our way home. I was thinking of The Greg in the house boat and smiling. It is usually me who ends up in the mire but for once I was let off. I wonder what the outcome would have been if I had decided to go Friday night with The Greg.

Stan dropped me off and was delighted that I gave him my wigeon. I would have loved to have eaten it myself. They are nearly as good as partridge. I walked into the house and my wife greeted me with, *"I hope there is nothing to cook."* I replied, *"Don't worry dear, you don't have to put yourself out this time."*

During the next week I was busy trying to arrange a small shooting party to visit Pontoon Wash. Because of prior commitments and Christmas being close, it wasn't possible to arrange a trip until January. I rang the gun shop in Wisbech for permits. Unfortunately the cabin on Pontoon Wash was fully booked for January. There were a couple of days free on Willow Wash so I booked them.

I asked Tony Wallace to join me and The Greg. Tony was working on the days I had booked but emphasised that he would like to join us another time. It was going to be just me and The Greg. I liked the look of Chatteris when we visited it and suggested to The Greg that we stayed there overnight. After being caught out before with dreadful accommodation, I thought it would be a good idea to have a look at where we were going to stay. The following Sunday we set off in The Greg's new racing car heading for Chatteris to carry out some reconnaissance work.

The Greg had changed his job and was now selling copying machines and office equipment. He was a first class salesman. If you can imagine this oversized extrovert, with a mop of red hair and full beard to match, stomping around your office trying to convince you that you would be a fool not to take up this once in a lifetime offer he was making you. I am sure most of the sales resulted from the clients fear of him, or the pure fact that he was far too big to throw out. He had me in stitches laughing at his stories.

We pulled into a small garage for some petrol. There were only two pumps and a car was parked across both of the pumps while the driver was filling the tank. The Greg pulled up behind the car to wait for it to move. The man filled his petrol tank and slowly replaced the nozzle of the pump and his petrol cap. He then casually strolled into the kiosk to pay for his petrol. The Greg started tapping his steering wheel. He wasn't the most patient man I have known. After chatting with the cashier for five minutes the man strolled out again never once looking at The Greg who by now had steam coming out of his ears. Things got worse! The stupid man walked round to the front of his car, lifted the bonnet and started to dip the oil. The Greg wound down his window and blasted his horn. The man looked out from under his bonnet. The Greg shouted, *"Could you move the car forward so I can get some petrol?"* The man just ignored him and carried on with his job. The Greg blasted his horn again. The man looked out again. *"If you don't bloody well move your car, I will move it for you."* This incredibly stupid man just ignored him again and bent back under the bonnet. That was it! The Greg put his car into gear and ran straight into the back of the other car. The car bonnet fell down on top of the occupant who eventually struggled out from under it and set off towards The Greg. With that The Greg jumped out of the car and stood there like a giant. The man stopped in his tracks. This red haired monster would have gobbled him up. He leapt into his car and sped off with the bonnet rattling. The Greg shrugged his shoulders and filled up with petrol. When he went to pay for his petrol the man in the kiosk was laughing. *"I am glad you did that."* he said, *"That arrogant bastard comes in here twice a week and blocks the pumps for twenty minutes while he goes through the same routine."* The Greg said it was a pity he had driven off as he would of liked to have throttled him. He followed this with a statement that it didn't matter about the dent in the front bumper as it was just a company car.

    We stopped at Mepal on the way to visit Albert in The Three Pickerels. It was freezing. The hardy Sunday lunch time locals were in there. They were sat playing dominoes in their overcoats, hats, scarves and fingerless gloves. The Greg wandered up to the bar. *"Hello Albert! Two pints of bitter with no ice please."* Albert smiled and asked The Greg if he had come to go sailing. This brought a roar of laughter from the domino school. Albert had obviously told them all the story. I was thinking of Pontoon Wash and what a long walk it was along the track. I asked Albert how do they transport the Calor Gas to the cabin. He told us they take it up in a Landrover early on in the season, before the rain and cattle have made the track impassable. He said it was usually driveable until the middle of November, depending on the weather.

    We had another pint and a game of dominoes against a couple of farmers. After a long game we beat them and The Greg held his hand out for the winnings. *"We don't normally pay strangers if they win in here."* stated one of the farmers. The Greg glared at him and said, *"Do you normally spend Christmas in hospital?"* The farmer paid up and we were on our way to Chatteris.

On the way we were discussing the shooting on the Ouse Washes. The Greg said we should try and find out when the grazing is auctioned so we could bid for the shooting on one of the washes. *"We should have asked Albert,"* he said, *"We had better call there on the way home tonight."* The Greg had taken to Albert in a strange sort of way. He certainly took every opportunity to visit.

We arrived at Chatteris and had a drive around. The place had a feeling of peace about it. Beautiful old buildings that looked as though they had been well lived in but not abused. We wanted a decent hotel but not too expensive. It is incredible what some people will pay to put their heads down for a night. If I was paying three hundred pounds a night I would refuse to go to sleep.

We found a nice looking hotel and in the window was a notice that gave the tariffs. A little more than we wanted to pay but it looked good. We decided to have a meal there and then make up our minds. It was an excellent meal of the chefs home made meat pie. The nearest I have ever had to how my dear mother made it. We were shooting for two days. Driving up early in the morning to shoot morning flight. Then into Greasy Joe's for breakfast followed by a visit to The Three Pickerels for dominoes. Back to Willow Wash to shoot evening flight and on to the hotel for a meal, a few drinks, a good night's sleep and up early for morning flight again. I was really pleased that I had taken the time to get the accommodation right after the disastrous trip to The Wash. We booked our rooms. The only drawback was the hotel didn't have kennels. *Lisa* would have to sleep in the car.

On the way back we stopped at The Three Pickerels. Albert gave us the information we needed. The auctions were held in The Three Pickerels at the beginning of May. The Greg sat down at a table and tipped the dominoes out of the box. I went to the bar and brought back a pint of bitter and a can of coke. The Greg looked at me in surprise and said, *"Who's drinking the coke?"* I replied quite firmly, *"The driver."* The Greg looked at me for a few seconds. He then pulled the keys out of his pocket and tossed them to me and said, *"Enjoy your coke!"* and carried on shuffling the dominoes. I was delighted. I would much rather drive than be driven by The Greg even when he is sober. Two hours later the car just purred along going home. I am sure it appreciated some gentle handling and not being used as a battering ram. The Greg slept most of the way. The small part of his face that wasn't covered with red whiskers looked totally contented. What an amazing character he was. Nothing ever bothered him for long.

I arrived home about half past eleven. The house was in darkness apart from the porch light. My wife and the children were in bed. There was a note on the table informing me that Tony Wallace had rung at nine. He wanted me to ring him back. I was contemplating whether I should ring him with it being so late, when the phone rang. It was Tony. He told me he had been out shooting pigeons that were coming into some stubble fields. He was off work for a couple of days. Would I like to have a shot at the pigeon in the morning? I had to make a decision. Will I go to work tomorrow or will I go pigeon shooting. It took me all of five seconds to thank him and say, *"What time shall I be there?"* Tony told me about nine and said goodnight.

I had a cup of tea and reflected on the day. *Lisa* sat next to me with her head on my knee. I was telling *Lisa* about the pigeon shooting tomorrow and her tail was wagging. The sitting room door opened and my wife walked in. *"I thought you had company, I heard you talking."* I told her I did have company. I had *Lisa* and I was talking to her. *"You are round the bloody twist!"* she stated, as she slammed the door on her way out.

Next morning at eight-thirty, me and *Lisa* were on our way to Letchworth. I was thinking to myself, I could enjoy being rich, being able to do what you want, when you want to. Having to work to earn enough money to survive is a pain in the rectum.

I had my Miroku twelve bore with me and fifty cartridges, arriving at Tony's house just before nine. He was at the gate waiting for me, rolling a cigarette, just the same as the last time I was there. *"Come and see Pat and have a cup of tea,"* he said. I followed him down the path. In the kitchen Pat was busy kneading some dough for the home made bread. This fellow is so fortunate. The only dough my wife is interested in is what she can extract out of me. Tony made some tea and started telling me about the pigeons. I asked him if he always shot on his days off. He told me he sometimes works helping a fencing contractor. I said the extra money would probably be handy. He said it would if he were to give me some but he usually pays me with dogs. After that statement he walked out. Pat said, *"He has just gone to the kennel at the bottom of the garden. We have got a new pup."* Tony returned with a Springer spaniel puppy about three months old. As he held the puppy up he said, *"Let me introduce you to Grobally, my latest payment from the fencing contractor."* Although this pup was only three months old it was nearly as big as *Lisa*. It had a face like a Bloodhound with enough spare folds of skin to grow into the size of a horse. The pup was more interested in getting stuck in to the ball of dough which Pat was still pushing around the kitchen table and it took Tony all his time to hold him. I said to Tony, *"He's a bit lively!"* The pup swung his head round and looked straight at me. I can tell you, if looks could kill that would have been the end of me. I have never seen a dog with so much facial expression. This puppy turned out to be a first class gun dog of tremendous character entertaining us for the next ten years with his antics and his attitude. He took a leading rôle in many of our wildfowling trips and you will see that he is mentioned in many of the stories. Tony took Grobally to the kennel and came back with a black Labrador. Pat said, *"I see you're going to take Brady."* *"Yes, I will take him,"* said Tony, *"He's no bloody use but he enjoys the walk."* Tony threw a rucksack on his back and picked up his gun which was standing in the corner in its sleeve. We said goodbye to Pat and went outside. Tony threw another sack on his back and set off down the path with Brady at his heel. *"Leave your car here!"* he said. *"We will walk."* I quickly got ready and we set off. We went about fifty yards up the road and through a gap between two houses on the opposite side. To my amazement we were straight into fields. After walking along a track for about half a mile, we cut off and crossed three fields to walk alongside a high hedgerow. *Lisa* suddenly dived into the hedge and flushed a very angry cock pheasant. The field this hedgerow was bordering was massive and was still in barley stubble. There were quite a lot of pigeon flying around and I wondered if we should have been out earlier. We came to a bend in the hedgerow which formed a kind of dog's leg in the field and Tony stopped. *"We will wait in here and put out some decoys,"* he said. He went through a gap into the hedge and I followed him. He had made a hide in there the day before. It was perfect! Being positioned on the bend in the hedge it allowed us to shoot from it at different angles making it safe. Brady turned around three times, laid down and went to sleep. Tony told me that Brady had absolutely no interest whatsoever in shooting or hunting. It was such a shame because he was a well built dog and really looked the part. He had been a payment for some work that Tony had carried out for the fencing contractor.

After walking out about thirty yards into the field Tony tipped out the contents of the sack he had been carrying. Twenty-five pigeons he had shot the day before. He told me that the pigeons had been hung in his shed overnight and he had put them in the sack that morning. He was taking them and any others we shot to the game dealer later in the day. We set them out in formation propping some of the heads up with twigs and returned to the hide. *Lisa* sat in the bottom of the hedge looking out across the field and it wasn't long before her tail was wagging. There were pigeon flying over the field most of the time. Every few minutes some of them came to the decoys offering good shooting. We kept running out propping up more pigeon. The decoy pattern was looking really impressive and the shooting was constant for about two hours. Tony looked at his watch and said, *"It's half past one, it will go quiet for an hour so we will have something to eat."* We had our sandwiches and a flask of coffee. It's strange how Brady slept through the shooting but as soon as we rustled a piece of paper that the sandwiches were in, he immediately woke up and produced that, poor me begging look, that dogs seem to be very good at. The last sandwich was shared between Brady and *Lisa*. That was the excitement over for Brady and he went back to sleep again. I know that the dogs have very little to do when decoying pigeon but occasionally a bird is hit and keeps flying only to drop out of the sky two fields away. That's when a good dog is useful.

Tony was right. After about an hour the action started again. Tony put his gun away and said he had run out of cartridges. I offered to share mine but he wouldn't take them. Instead he produced a cine-camera from his bag and started to film me shooting at the pigeons coming in and swinging over the decoys. Once I new I was being filmed it is incredible how my shooting deteriorated. When Tony run out of film I started to hit them again. At a quarter to four I had used all my cartridges and we collected the birds. Forty-five pigeons had been shot over the decoys and one that *Lisa* brought back from the next field. I carried them to the edge of a road which was two fields away. Tony went back home and brought his jeep. We took them to the game dealer and then returned to Tony's house. As before Pat provided fresh warm bread with plenty of butter and cheese all washed down with hot mugs of tea. That was the first of many days me and Tony spent culling the pigeon population with the best days shooting to come over freshly sown peas.

Christmas and New Year passed by and thank goodness for that. I enjoyed Christmas when the children were small but it just doesn't seem the same now. I usually shoot on Boxing Day so that's a bonus. I managed to talk The Greg into leaving his new racing car at home and travel to the washes with me. I didn't think my nerves could stand another journey in his car I hadn't recovered from the last one.

The time had come and I drove to The Greg's house at three in the morning. Getting out of the car and closing the door quietly not wanting to waken the neighbours at such an unearthly hour. The Greg came out of the front door of the house shouting and laughing in his usual way. No consideration for the neighbours at all. He probably hadn't even noticed that he had neighbours. Two or three slams of the boot and the doors and we were on our way. The weather was dreadful with strong wind and heavy rain. The windscreen wipers on double speed most of the way. As we drove through Baldock a policeman stepped out in the road in front of us and waved a red torch towards the side of the road making a gesture for me to stop. If The Greg had been driving the stupid policeman would have been mincemeat. He came to the side of the car and bent over to speak to me. I wound down the window and *Lisa* growled at him. I didn't know she disliked policemen. That was the first time I had heard her growl. The policeman looked cautiously at the dog and said. *"Good evening sir! just a routine check. Are you the owner of this car?"* I told him I was and The Greg stated. *"If we were going to steal a car my friend we would steal a better one than this."* The policeman shone his torch on The Greg for a few seconds but didn't reply. He just stood there bent over with the rain pouring off his helmet. *"I would like to look in the boot,"* he said. I told him to help himself, it wasn't locked. He walked round to the back of the car and lifted the boot for a few minutes and then closed it. Returning to the window he asked. *"Why have you got two guns in the boot?"* The Greg replied before I had the chance. *"We are going to do an armed robbery and the dog is going to be the lookout."* The policeman took a deep breath ready to read us the riot act but I managed to speak before him. I told him we were going duck shooting and had to be there before daybreak. If we didn't get going soon we were going to be late. After I produced my documents he reluctantly let us proceed on our journey. *"What a pillock!"* The Greg stated, *"stopping us on a night like this and standing out there in the bloody rain."* The Greg laughed when I pointed out to him that he may be a pillock but at least he is being paid for being out there. We are going out there for the pleasure.

We arrived at Mepal without any further incidents an hour before daybreak. The weather was atrocious. I was quite happy with the strong wind but we could have done without the heavy rain. Soon ready with waders and waterproofs we were on our way. The track was slippery and the wind and rain were driving straight into our faces. Over the past month I had grown a beard which gave some protection but nothing like the beard The Greg always had. Nothing could penetrate that. After three quarters of an hour of slipping and cursing we reached The Greg's beloved house boat and crossed the little bridge onto Willow Wash. What a difference to last time! The whole wash was covered in water. I could make out the hides which we had used previously sticking out of the water. I told The Greg that we will have to be careful that we don't end up in the ponds. It was a good thing that we were here before the wash had flooded at least we new there was a potential danger there. There were some small trees in the middle of the wash and we headed for them walking in about nine inches of water. When we arrived there I was pleased to see it was like an island and the water was only three inches deep. That was going to make things a lot easier for *Lisa*. Positioning ourselves forty yards apart, both behind a little tree, we waited for daybreak. The rain had eased off but the wind was getting stronger. I was excited. The conditions were good for duck shooting, let's hope the ducks think so as well.

Light was starting to break but it was a very dark cloudy sky making it difficult to see. I heard a pack of wigeon go over but was frustrated not being able to see them. *Lisa* had seen them and looked at me in disgust. A few minutes later another pack and The Greg's gun was in action. It was still so dark that I saw the flash out of the gun's barrels. The famous shout came next from The Greg. *"Fetch your dog."* I shouted I would come later and waited for the next pack. I didn't have long to wait. Six mallard flew over me with the wind up their bums. I poked the gun and missed with both barrels. After giving myself a good telling off for not swinging the gun I settled again. It was a lot lighter when the next pack of wigeon came. There must have been over two hundred of them at about thirty yards screaming over the top of us. We both took out a right and left. The Greg squealed a *"Yahoo!"* at the top of his voice with excitement. Before it was full daylight I had shot another three wigeon and The Greg had shot two. The wigeon kept coming in their droves. Unfortunately, as it became full light they were flying a good twenty yards higher. I have seen wigeon shot at that height but more often than not they are just pricked only to fly on and suffer a slow death from gangrene. We stood and watched them for half an hour but they seemed to be flying higher. I began to realise just how cold my feet were. It's strange how you don't notice when the adrenaline is flowing. *Lisa* had been busy picking up and didn't seem to notice the cold. We walked back to the wood which was above the water level and watched the flight. I didn't know where they were coming from or where they were going but every five minutes or so a pack of wigeon of anything between twenty and a hundred flew down the wash on the same flight line at the same height. This is something I am going to investigate I thought. At ten we walked back down the track in good spirits with the wind at our backs and were soon at the car. I gave *Lisa* a good rub down with a towel then we were heading for Greasy Joe's.

Enjoying a good breakfast we reflected on the day so far. The rain had blown away and the sky was clearing. It was definitely feeling colder. The Greg ordered two more mugs of tea and I took a sausage sandwich out for *Lisa* which pleased her immensely. Back in Greasy Joe's we were talking about the wigeon we had seen it was incredible how many there were. I had heard there was a place called Welney where there was a reserve for wildfowl. On the map you could see that Welney was on the washes about ten miles from Mepal as the wigeon fly. We decided to investigate and drove to Welney. There is a vast reserve there run by The Wildfowl & Wetlands Trust. This must be where the wigeon were flighting from. It would be between eight and nine miles to Willow Wash from there and the speed the wigeon were going this morning it wouldn't take them very long to travel to it.

Curiosity satisfied we drove back to Mepal and spent a few hours with Albert in The Three Pickerels. A couple of farmers came in and sat at a table drinking a pint while looking at some papers. We were propping up the bar talking to Albert when he told us these farmers bid for the grazing on the washes. I asked Albert if he would introduce us to them with the prospect of leasing some shooting for the following season. Albert shouted across to the farmers. *"I have a couple of wildflowers here who want to lease some shooting for next season."* One of the farmers looked across and said, *"Be in here the first Thursday evening in May and we will see what we can do."* I thanked them and bought them a pint.

It didn't seem long that we had been in the pub when Albert was putting the towels on the pumps. Half past two already. The Greg tried to talk Albert into giving him another pint but Albert was adamant that he needed to clear up after we had gone ready for opening this evening. The Greg was quick to point out that there had only been four people in the place so it wouldn't need that much cleaning. Albert told him to come back at six if he wanted another pint. The Greg muttered something into his glass as he was finishing off the dregs and we left.

With a nice steady walk we returned to Willow Wash. Standing at the edge of the wood we were reasonably well sheltered. The washes were separated by fences that were constructed with posts and sheep netting with a row of barbed wire at the top. Farmers just love barbed wire. I have ripped more clothes and waterproof equipment on barbed wire than I care to remember. Even worse I have seen dogs with great gashes torn in their bellies by the damned stuff.

I was once beating on an estate in Scotland called Kildonan. I got caught up by the crutch on a barbed wire fence when I tried to cross it. A Member of Parliament was one of the guest guns on the day and he kindly rescued me. A little while later this M. P. was given a peerage and he had to choose a title. I am not certain what title he chose but he was affectionately named by the beaters as, 'Lord Scrotum of Kildonan'.

Lisa kept standing up on her back legs looking towards the fence and whining. There was certainly something she had noticed in the water caught up in the wire fence. She wanted to go so I sent her. Jumping through the water some of the way and swimming when she crossed the hidden pond she went out about a hundred yards coming back with a cock wigeon. It wasn't shot today we had picked everything this morning. Because it was still fresh we assumed it had been shot the day before. This find was interesting and the dog enjoyed it. There were other washes either side of Willow Wash. I wondered if there could be any more ducks caught up on the dividing fences. I left my gun with The Greg and took a pair of binoculars out of my bag. Walking back along the track with *Lisa* we came to the dividing fence of the wash below us. I looked along it through the binoculars. The grass had grown through the fence in great tufts. There was something caught up in the grass so I sent *Lisa*. She ploughed through the water alongside the fence coming back with another cock wigeon. Delivering it to me she went back to the clump of grass. I saw her head go right under the water and out it came with another wigeon which turned out to be a hen. Both of the birds were fresh. There must have been a shooting party out the day before without dogs. The birds had been blown on the water to the fence where they got caught in the grass and wire. I find it incredible that people turn out for a days shooting without a dog. One of the main pleasures of the day is watching the dog work. The Greg had a useless dog called Winston for a while until he gave it away. He never bothered to replace it. God knows how many ducks and pheasants The Greg would have lost if it hadn't been for the efforts of *Lisa*.

I walked back to The Greg were we were greeted with a round of applause for *Lisa*. I asked him if he had thought of getting another dog after giving Winston away. He said he had thought about it but was frightened he would end up with another wassock like Winston.

I firmly believe there is no such thing as a bad dog. Ninety-nine percent of the time its the owners who haven't got a clue or the dog has been to old before someone tried to train it. I believe that when you acquire a puppy you must spend lots of time with it. I know some people say you should put them in a kennel and leave them until they are old enough to train. I don't think you should rush a puppy into training but you must build up a bond of friendship with it. You have to love and respect it and it will reciprocate. Some puppies take longer than others to form this bond but once it is there all that puppy will ever want to do is please you. The more obedient it becomes the more it pleases you and the puppy soon realises this. When training a puppy every time it does something right I make a tremendous fuss of it. If it does something wrong I speak to it in a firm voice but most important I ignore it for ten minutes. This really hurts them because you are their best friend. They feel secure having a friend and they don't want to lose your friendship. Before long you start to work as a team and the pleasures from that are indescribable. I have two Springer spaniels now called Meg and Bess. They are both good workers and my best friends. I can't imagine living without dogs. They live in the house and are totally spoilt. Yet on a shooting day they are there working away with the one ambition of pleasing me. The sadness is their short life span. Over the years I have been heartbroken on too many occasions when I have had to say farewell to a good close friend.

We set out our stall for evening flight making proper hides out of the small trees. Nothing much happened until it was nearly dark when some pintail flew over us and we managed to shoot one each. There was no sign of the wigeon. I don't know where they had gone to in the morning but they certainly were not returning. When it was nearly dark we saw the most spectacular sight. A flight of over a hundred Bewick Swans flew over our heads at no more than fifteen yards up. You could feel the draught from their wings. I heard them drop in on the next wash. As we were walking back we could hear them talking away to each other. A sound that most people will never hear in their lifetime. What a pleasure just to witness it.

Back to the car and time to dry *Lisa* and give her some dinner. She looked at me and wagged her tail as if to say thank you. The Greg wanted to go in and see Albert but I talked him out of it. I was ready for a shower and a good meal.

The lights on the hotel at Chatteris looked welcoming. I parked in the car park at the back of the hotel and covered *Lisa* up with some blankets. She was quite happy and went straight to sleep. We took our guns in and were shown to our rooms. The curtains were already drawn and the room was warm and cosy. I took some polythene out of my bag and lay it on the carpet. I then lay an old bath towel I had brought with me on the polythene. I now had somewhere to clean my gun. Once staying in a hotel with a shooting party I witnessed a man, who shall be nameless, clean his gun on the bed and then wipe off the excess oil with the underside of the bed covers. Is there any wonder that some hotels will not accommodate wildfowlers? After a hot shower I put on some decent clothes and went downstairs. I wasn't surprised to find The Greg in the bar chatting away to the barman. Having swallowed a couple of beers we went to the dining room for dinner. Taking our time over a four course meal with a bottle of wine we really enjoyed it. During our meal we were discussing wigeon and dogs and if only those swans had been geese. Back into the bar about nine for a night-cap and then an early night. The bar was filling up with youths who were getting a bit noisy. I decided it was bedtime and went to my room a couple of minutes after ten.

Into the pyjamas, light out and into bed. Wonderful! I was just dropping off when the luck of the Raw struck. I heard something that made me nearly jump out of my bloody skin. 'Bong Bong,'

'Bong Bong'. I leapt out of bed and pulled back the curtains. I couldn't believe it. The bloody room was opposite Big Ben. The clock proceeded to chime every fifteen minutes through the night only to stop on the hour and blast out a bloody big 'Bong' for every hour that had passed. I could see my car below in the car park and thought of *Lisa*. I climbed back into bed to wait for the next blast from the clock. Putting a pillow over my ears I managed to drop off to sleep only to be wakened by a rumpus going on outside. I switched the light on and looked at my watch. It was twenty past twelve. The noise was coming from the car park. I looked out of the window and there were half a dozen youths shouting and hollering while two more were knocking seven shades out of each other. They were right next to my car and I was concerned for *Lisa*. Opening the window I shouted down at them to keep away from my car. I received a mouthful of abuse that contained about ten effings. I am not a brave man but that dog meant the world to me and she must have been frightened having never witnessed violence before. I pulled my trousers on over my pyjamas and slipped into a pair of shoes. My gun was laid out on the towel still in pieces. I picked up the barrels, wrapped them in the towel and took them with me. After going down the corridor to The Greg's room I could hear his snores from outside. His door was locked. I tapped on the door but he snored on. Bugger it! I will have to go on my own. I went out the front door and into the street. I could have done with a policeman now. It's funny how they never seem to be there when you want them but they have a knack of turning up when you least want them. Running round the corner I went into the car park, which was illuminated from a light on the hotel wall. Thank goodness most of the lunatics had gone but there were still three of them. Two of them were helping another one to his feet. They looked up and saw me. One of them screamed *"There's that bastard who shouted out of the window!"* The youth they had picked up looked as though he had been run over by a tram. His face was covered in blood and one eye had completely closed. They came towards me. When they were about five yards away I threw the towel off the barrels and held them up gripping them with both hands. The youth with the bloody face stopped when he saw me. I think he had enough for one night. The other two looked at each other and came towards me slowly. I shouted at them. *"Come on then boys if you want to, but I am telling you now, I am not going to hold back. Your faces will end up in the same state as your mate's."* They stopped and looked at each other again. The youth with the bloody face said. *"Come on John leave it, I want to get home."* They stepped back to their friend and helped him out of the car park. As they were going one of them turned around and said. *"We will sort you out tomorrow if you're still here."* I never answered. I was glad to see the back of them. I went to the car where *Lisa* was sat on the back seat looking out of the window at me. I let her out and she was pleased to see me. Deciding I wasn't going to leave her again I picked up the towel and went back to my room taking *Lisa* with me. Putting my gun together I placed it in its sleeve which had dried on the radiator. Laying the towel onto the polythene I made a bed for *Lisa* where she curled up contented and went to sleep. She was lucky! I never slept another wink. After all the planning another bloody disaster. At quarter to six I took *Lisa* back to the car and waited for breakfast in the dining room. The breakfast was on the table at six as promised. The Greg came down with a smile on his face. *"You can't beat a good night's sleep,"* he said, as he got stuck in to the first greasy breakfast of the day. I let him eat his breakfast and then I told him the story. *"Never heard a bloody thing,"* he said. *"It's a good job you never bent your barrels."* In a way I wished I had. I hope my children never grow up to be like those youths. I am sure it is probably the same with children as it is with puppies. Once you have obtained their love and respect there should be no problems. I smuggled a sausage and a slice of bacon out in a napkin for *Lisa*. She gobbled them down and licked her lips.

 Driving back to Mepal it was cold and windy outside. There had been a frost overnight and the roads looked glassy. I was still annoyed about the previous night and not concentrating on my driving when I hit a patch of black ice. The car did a complete spin. There was nobody else on the road so I was lucky and managed to gain control of the car. The Greg roared with laughing. *"That's what happens when you drive slow,"* he said. I didn't answer him. I couldn't see the funny side of it. I was thinking to myself how much I am looking forward to staying in the cabin at Pontoon Wash. At least it hasn't got Big Ben outside.

 Parking up in the Pickerels car park we were off again up the muddy track. As we got closer to the wash we could here the swans. They were still chattering away. Taking up position in the hides we had built the previous day we waited. The noise from the swans was getting louder. You could sense the excitement among them. The light was just breaking when they lifted. They sound incredibly like geese and an inexperienced wildfowler could be forgiven for mistaking the calls. They came back towards us fighting against the wind. As they flew over they were only five yards high gaining height as they went. I wished I had brought a camera as well as the gun it was a wonderful moment.

The wigeon flight followed and we shot two each. As the day broke the weather changed. The wind was losing its strength and it was getting warmer. The sun was rising and it was more like a spring morning. We walked back down the track and I must admit I was buggered. When we were eating our second breakfast in Greasy Joe's I told The Greg I was tired, and happy with what I had shot. I indicated I wouldn't mind heading homewards. The Greg didn't mind missing the evening flight because the weather had changed. He suggested just one more visit to Albert's and we will be on our way. I reluctantly agreed and we were home for tea time. I had a bath and went straight to bed sleeping right through till the following morning. When I was driving to work I was thinking of the swans. Where will they be today? Probably at Welney eating breakfast.

CHAPTER 6

First trip to Pontoon Wash

The first trip to the cabin was with The Greg and a friend of his called Sandy. It is not like The Greg to suffer fools but this lunatic was beyond a joke. The Greg must have seen something in Sandy that I couldn't because he seemed to like him. I have met a few people like Sandy over the years. It is hard to explain exactly what I mean but they are the sort of people who are constantly heading for disasters. They never listen to anyone who warns them of their potential outcome, they just plod on until it happens. When the disaster has happened they shrug their shoulders and start a fresh course to another disaster not learning anything at all from their previous mistakes.

It was very early in the season at the end of September when we decided to have a break from the real world and hide away on the Ouse Washes for a few days. Tony had to work and missed out again. I have always stated that work is the curse of the drinking classes. We were travelling to Mepal on the Sunday and returning to the real world on Tuesday night.

The Greg was coming in my car, thank goodness. His car was in for repair after he had smashed the front in trying to run someone off the road. We had to attend a committee meeting on the Sunday morning for the clay pigeon club and we were to travel to the Ouse Washes after that had finished. Sandy was making his own way there and The Greg had given him directions. We loaded up the car with all the gear before the meeting started. The heaviest containers being enough water to last us for three days and a bottle of whisky and gin in case we got fed up with water.

The meeting dragged on a bit which pleased The Greg because it was being held in a pub and at twelve they opened the bar. When ever I want to get away there is always somebody who wants to debate something that is not only stupid, but totally irrelevant to what we had been discussing. I have found that most of the people who join committees only join so they can hear themselves speak. It doesn't seem to matter to them that they are speaking a load of twaddle. They are probably hen pecked at home and this is their only chance of expressing themselves.

Eventually the meeting was closed and I managed to prise The Greg out of the bar. I stopped at my house to collect *Lisa*. She knew something was going on when I was loading the car earlier that morning and she looked extremely sad when I drove off to the meeting without her. When I pulled up outside the house she was sat looking out of the window. The delight on her face when she saw me said everything. By the time I had reached the front door she was there with her tail wagging so fast that she was cooling the hall. Guns and cartridges loaded and we were on our way.

It was a quiet journey there. The Greg fell asleep after ten minutes and didn't wake up until I pulled up outside The Three Pickerels at Mepal. He looked at his watch and was disappointed to find that the pub was closed. We were hoping that the track up to Pontoon Wash would be dry enough to drive the car to the cabin, saving a long walk with all our equipment. We parked in the pub car park and walked over the bridge to the gate which is the entrance to the track leading to the washes. The gate was open and just inside the gate was the great pond of soft mud we had seen the previous January. The rest of the field and the main track wasn't too bad and we decided to risk driving to the cabin. The Greg held the gate and I brought the car across, driving through the opening and keeping tight to the right avoiding the pond of mud. I managed to keep the car moving until I was on top of the embankment of the Hundred Foot River where I stopped to wait for The Greg who had shut the gate after I had driven in. Most of the track was firm but we had a few anxious moments where it was slippery and the back end of the Cortina Estate tried to slide down the steep bank. With more luck than judgement I managed to keep going and we soon arrived at the cabin.

Sandy was already there and his Mini Cooper was parked on the track. *Lisa* was really excited and was quite happy to start work immediately as she flushed a pheasant from some bushes at the bottom of the bank. I went up the steps at the side of the cabin leading onto the balcony and looked over the whole of Pontoon Wash. The grass was thick about eighteen inches high but there was still plenty of water in the ponds. I looked through my binoculars and could see teal on the pond at the far side of the wash. The site of these ducks sent butterflies through my stomach. I went through the door from the balcony into the cabin. Sandy was busy pouring some tea into mugs and said. *"How many sugars Vince?"* I told him none and he handed me a mug of tea. I looked at it suspiciously. It appeared to have insects floating in it. I asked him if he had brought the water with him. He said, *"No, there is a little pump on the tap over the sink. I just pumped it and out came the water."* I went out onto the balcony and down the steps to investigate.

The pipe from the gutter that discharged the water from the cabin roof was fixed into a rusty old tank. The water in the tank was dirty and full of aquatic life. There was a plastic pipe positioned vertically out of the water connected to the pump that Sandy had been operating. That stupid bastard could have poisoned us all and we would have laid there until Wednesday before anyone would have missed us. I am sure that during the winter months when there is plenty of rain the water might well be useful for washing up, when it had been boiled. After carrying the water, weighing ten pounds a gallon, up the muddy track for well over two miles, the last thing you want to use it for would be washing up. I am sure the pump was a good idea. It just goes to show what can go wrong when you have got an idiot in the camp.

I carried my gear into the cabin and selected a lower bunk for sleeping. *Lisa* would like that because she could sleep on the floor next to the bunk. I still had my decent clothes on from attending the meeting earlier and was tempted to change. The Greg said, *"Don't bother changing. By the time we have had something to eat The Three Pickerels will be open and we can go and see Albert, the landlord."* I don't know why I listen to him, I usually regret it.

When we were eating I asked Sandy how his Mini coped with the slippery track. He replied, *"No trouble at all! Mini's are brilliant in these conditions."* I then asked him if he had left the gate open. *"Yes, I decided to keep going once I was through the gate. I knew you were coming in later."* There are times when it is better for me to keep quiet because I can get so angry with plonkers like him, it is bad for my blood pressure.

When we had finished eating and sorted our equipment out it was time to visit Albert. I was quite looking forward to seeing him again. Sandy said we could go in his Mini. To avoid obstructing the track, I drove my car over the little bridge onto the wash. The Mini was good in the conditions but I am sure it would have been far more comfortable if Sandy had reduced the speed by half. I told him to stop on the top of the embankment and The Greg went down and opened the gate. Sandy then drove down the bank, round the pond of mud, through the gate and into The Three Pickerels car park. Maybe I had misjudged him, at least he got that right.

Albert greeted us immediately with his usual sarcasm. *"Come on in you must be the best dressed wildflowers in town."* I told him we like to dress for the occasion as we didn't want to be shown up by his usual clientele. Albert laughed. Give him is due, he can take it as well as dishing it out. The Greg bought a round of drinks. A pint each for me and him and Sandy said, *"I think I will have a brandy."* The Greg said, *"Think again and think beer."* Sandy settled for a pint and went and sat down on his own. Me and The Greg were talking to Albert. He was going through his card tricks and loving every minute of having a fresh audience. The place was slightly warmer than the last time we were there, but not much. I said to Albert, *"It seems warmer in here. Have you put a shilling in the meter?"* Albert said, *"If you are too warm I will open the window."* This brought a roar of laughter.

After a while I bought a round including a brandy for Sandy. Me and The Greg started a game of dominoes. A game of fives and three's can go on a long time with The Greg so I found a comfortable chair out of the draught. Half an hour later all our glasses were empty and Sandy just sat there watching us play dominoes. Eventually The Greg said to him, *"Are you going to buy a round Sandy?"* Sandy replied, *"No, I haven't brought any money with me."* I was beginning to dislike Sandy even more. I have met his sort before. They are quite happy to take a drink off everybody with no intentions of reciprocating. When it is their turn to buy a round they usually vanish to the toilet or sneak off home. What really annoys me is not the cost, but the fact that they think you are so stupid that you haven't even noticed their little plan. The Greg gave Sandy ten pounds and Sandy returned with two pints and a brandy for himself. He handed the change to The Greg. The Greg said, *"Keep the change. You owe me ten pounds."* Sandy looked horrified. That was probably the first round he had ever bought.

It was soon time to say goodnight to Albert. He left us with the remark, *"Goodnight, my well dressed wildflowers and sleep tight in that shed."* He plugs away calling us wildflowers. I climbed into the front seat of the Mini next to Sandy and The Greg went across the road to open the gate. I said to Sandy, *"Drive through the gate and keep to the right, then wait on the top of the embankment for The Greg."* He replied, *"I know! I am not stupid."* I could have argued that point but kept quiet.

It is amazing how people turn into racing drivers when they have had a taste of alcohol. The Greg had opened the gate and we set off out of the car park in the Mini Cooper as though somebody had just given us the green light at Brands Hatch. Sandy pushed the accelerator hard down onto the floor and we drove over the bridge and through the gate with the wheels spinning. He swung the steering wheel to the right, but the car was going far too fast for the wheels to grip the ground and it carried on sideways straight into the pond of mud. I sat there in disbelief. How could anyone be so bloody stupid? We were in the middle of the pond just floating on the mud and he was revving the engine trying to blow it up. I was lost for words and decided I would kill him. When it was obvious the car wasn't going anywhere The Greg took his shoes off and waded into the mud. He managed to push the floating car towards the edge but not close enough for the wheels to grip. There was no alternative. I would have to get out. The Greg said be careful I think I have cut my foot. I decided to leave my shoes on as they would clean later and stepped out of the car into two feet of cold slimy mud. With a joint effort, me and The Greg managed to slowly move the car forward, while the plonker was sat in it, bone dry. With the last heave the front wheels gripped and the car shot forward leaving me tumbling face down into the mud. When I managed to stagger out I realised I had lost my shoes. *Lisa* had been sat on the back seat watching this performance. I would love to know what she was thinking. Climbing back into the Mini I was pleased to spread as much mud around the upholstery as possible.

Back at the cabin I took all my clothes off and put them into a dustbin bag ready for taking home. Climbing into my bunk I decided to plan the best way of killing Sandy. My thoughts soon reverted to duck flighting and it wasn't long before I was nodding with my arm around *Lisa*.

It was a cold nose in my face that woke me at five in the morning, followed by an affectionate lick, and I am not referring to Sandy. It was great to wake up to be going duck shooting instead of going to work. Getting dressed I put the kettle on for some tea before going out onto the balcony. It was wonderful to be out there away from the every day hustle and bustle, listening to the world of the wildlife that goes on when we are asleep.

It was still long before dawn, but not that dark. I have shot ducks in similar light, with a fleecy kind of sky. Becoming restless I wanted to be out there. Going back into the cabin I made three pots of tea. Whilst I was drinking mine, I was putting my waders and

A cold nose in my face followed by an affectionate lick.

jacket on getting ready to go. The Greg and Sandy didn't seem to be in any hurry so I told them I would see them later, and set off for the furthest pond, where I had seen the teal the day before.

It was a typical late September morning with a chill in the air, but not really cold. How I enjoyed those moments with just me and *Lisa*. What wonderful company that little dog was. We had been together for so long now we understood and relied on each other. In another three years she would be ready for retirement. It must be part of nature when a dog seems to know that it is ready to retire, letting a younger dog take its place in the field to carry out the work. They are quite happy to stay at home and curl up in front of the fire being totally spoilt by the family.

We settled in a makeshift hide by the pond and waited. Looking at my gun I started to think about my first gun. When I was thirteen, one of my friends offered to swap his air rifle for my football boots, which I had recently saved up to buy. I wasn't very good at football and to own a gun was something very special to me. I decided the best way to persuade my Father to allow this swap to happen, was through my Mother. I could talk to my Mother and she would listen and try to understand. I don't know what pressure she used on my Father, but whatever it was it worked, and I was allowed the gun. Setting up targets on the garden fence I started shooting. Everything went well until my hunting instinct got the better of me. I couldn't resist a shot at a starling flying over our neighbour's garden. I wished that I had missed it, but the luck of the Raw struck and I hit the damn thing. A total disaster! The poor starling was only injured and landed at the feet of our neighbour, who attracted the birds to his garden by feeding them. A few moments later he was standing at the door of our house. The wounded starling was in his hands and he was complaining bitterly to my Mother. My Father was told and he confiscated the gun.

My concentration was regained when I received the signal from *Lisa*. Her tail started to wag and a bunch of teal flew over the pond. I picked them out against the fleecy sky and took the last one out of the bunch. It came down in the grass at the other side of the pond so I sent *Lisa* to retrieve. She had a wise head and took the route around the pond. A younger dog learning its trade would have probably dived straight into the water. She was soon back with the teal without any fuss and ready for the next one. Some wigeon screamed over and I managed one barrel but missed about ten feet behind. More wigeon and I took one out. This was exciting and it still hadn't broken light.

Lisa looked up the wash towards the cabin and whined. I looked round and couldn't believe what I was seeing. One of the biggest spot lights I had ever seen was heading towards me, shining all over the place. As it came closer I realised it was the plonker. He wandered up and I asked him to turn the light off. He said, *"I heard the shooting so I thought I would join you."* He stood next to me for a few minutes and some mallard flew across the pond. He fired at them straight over my head and nearly deafened me. That was the last straw. I stood up and told him he could have my hide and I would find somewhere else. I then moved to a pond in the middle of the wash and waited there. It soon became light and I never fired another shot although I heard a couple from the plonker. After ten minutes of daylight he wandered over to me spoiling any chance of a shot and said, *"There is a duck down on the pond."* I asked him if it was dead. He said, *"Yes."* I told him to go in and get it, then he would find out what it is like to get wet. I set off back to the cabin for breakfast, with *Lisa* at my heel.

After a few minutes The Greg came into the cabin. I told him I wasn't pleased with Sandy. The Greg said that he had told Sandy to stay near him, but he had wandered off. Soon after Sandy came in. He said he hadn't managed to retrieve the duck and it didn't seem to concern him.

After breakfast I stood on the balcony and looked out. It was a beautiful day. Every so often a pack of wigeon flew over extremely high. The Greg was talking about going down to Greasy Joe's café and then to The Pickerels for lunch. All I wanted to do was sit by one of the ponds with *Lisa,* and enjoy the peace and quiet. The plonker was going to go with The Greg which suited me. At the last minute the plonker decided to stay and keep me company. I didn't believe this man. How much would I have to insult him before he got the message. I told him I wanted to sit by one of the ponds on my own. He said, *"Fair enough! I will sit by another one."* The Greg borrowed his Mini and drove away down the track.

I walked back to the furthest pond on the wash where I had been earlier. The duck that the plonker had shot was still in the middle. *Lisa* would have willingly retrieved it but I didn't want her to be wet all day when it wasn't necessary. She could fetch it later. I worked on the hide for half an hour and made a better seat with some branches and reeds. I watched the plonker go to another pond. He couldn't seem to settle. Every time I looked he was wandering around, walking backwards. I was puzzled as to why he was always walking backwards, but then decided there would be no logical reason for it, other than to annoy me. If any ducks decide to come to the ponds during the day he is certainly going to frighten them off.

I sat there stroking *Lisa* and thinking about dogs. The previous January I had bought a black Labrador bitch puppy and called her Sally. I was enjoying training her and looking forward to working her next season. I always have bitches. They are so much easier to work with than dogs. I find that they are more affectionate and therefore, it is easier to form the bond that is essential, if you are going to have a good working relationship. *Lisa* wasn't too impressed with the new arrival, but she had seen it all before.

I once went to Hinckley with a friend, to collect a Springer spaniel puppy he was buying. I came back with the three bitches that were left in the litter. They were brilliant puppies, off first class stock, and I just couldn't leave them behind. I lived at the foot of Dunstable Downs. The Downs proved to be an ideal place for training dogs. I sold the dogs at twelve months old when they were obedience trained, walking to heel, hunting, retrieving, dropping to shot and returning on the whistle. These puppies were so intelligent it was a pleasure to train them. I could have sold them ten times over for a lot of money but I was very selective about where they were going to spend the rest of their lives. I was happy letting them go to friends where I knew they would have a good home, and a full working life. They turned out to be first class dogs and I was proud to watch them work on many occasions.

The plonker was still walking about backwards when justice prevailed. He must have stepped back into a hole because he suddenly fell and vanished out of sight. The enjoyable part was, a great splash of water came up from where he had landed. I laughed and felt like cheering. *Lisa* gave me a look of pleasure and wagged her tail. The plonker wandered back to the cabin and stayed there.

Lisa gave me a look of pleasure and wagged her tail.

There was the odd pack of wigeon flighting over like dots in the sky but apart from that it was very quiet. In the middle of the afternoon I saw the grass moving on the other side of the pond. Sitting dead still I peeped out through my hide. A little while later some more movement, and a fox's head poked up out of the grass. Cautiously approaching the edge of the pond the fox started drinking. It was a big dog fox which was nearly red. He must have picked up the scent of the duck in the middle because it fixed its eyes on it. Unfortunately, he must also have picked up my scent, because he had a good look around and then slinked away through the grass. I am not an expert on foxes but I was always led to believe that they don't like to swim. They are quick to take advantage of a frozen pond, crossing on the ice to take an unsuspecting duck from the island, but it is very rare that they have been seen swimming. If that is the case, then how is this fox here? It is on a strip of land that is three quarters of a mile wide and twenty miles long, with a river on each side. From January to March the whole area will be flooded. I came to the conclusion, he either swam across one of the rivers or, he came in the gate which we used, opposite The Pickerels. There is one thing for certain, in a few months time he is going to have to find a way out, or be drowned. At the moment he will be living well eating ducks that have been shot by wildfowlers without dogs.

Getting stiff from sitting in the hide for so long, I decided to go back to the cabin and have a bite to eat before evening flight. I sent *Lisa* for Sandy's duck and we walked back. *Lisa* was amusing herself hunting the tufts of grass from which voles were running out in great numbers. The harriers and owls must find plenty to eat here.

As I was walking back I was feeling contented. This is far better than work. I would be happy to be here every day of the week. When I reached the cabin the Mini came up the track and skidded to a halt. The Greg squeezed out of the door with some difficulty and had a huge grin on his face. He asked *"Have you killed him yet?"* I told him, *"Not yet, but he has had a good soaking."* We went into the cabin and saw that Sandy was in his bunk. His clothes were over the chairs drying in front of the open oven, which was lit. It turned out that the plonker hadn't brought any spare clothes. The clothes that were drying were all he had. I immediately thought of stealing them, and then he would have to stay in the cabin. I stupidly gave him some spare clothes of mine and he got dressed.

The Greg was full of beer and food and didn't want anything more to eat. Heating a tin of sausage and beans I served it on toast and shared it with Sandy. Whilst we were eating I tried to nicely explain a few things to him. I told him how I have to work most days, building peoples houses and extensions, and how much I get stressed up doing it. I carried on to tell him, because of the stress I really look forward to my shooting trips, where I can relax and enjoy myself. The last thing I want is for someone to come along and spoil it for me. He carried on eating and said, *"I don't blame you!"* Not even realising that the remarks were aimed at him. I thought I have tried everything else. I will definitely have to kill him.

We had a cup of tea and I went back onto the balcony. Looking through my binoculars I saw the fox. He was back at the far pond probably checking to see if the duck was still there. He will have to put up with vole for his dinner tonight. I went back inside and asked Sandy where he would like to go for evening flight. Sandy said he didn't care, and The Greg offered to take him to where he had been in the morning. I didn't argue and as I was going out the door I said, *"Please leave the search light behind. I am going to the far pond."*

I was in the hide and daylight was fading. A pair of harriers were working away, totally oblivious to my presence. I had that feeling of satisfaction being so close to wild creatures without them being aware of me. They wouldn't have to work very hard to find their dinners, the place was running with voles. I heard two shots from the other ponds and seconds later a pack of wigeon came over my head. There must have been fifty in the pack and I am delighted to say, forty-eight flew out. I was really happy now, if I didn't fire another shot on this trip I wouldn't mind. I had shot a right and left at wigeon, and that's what duck shooting is all about.

There were another six shots from the other pond. I was busy watching the harriers when five pintail screamed over my head. I hit the one at the back and it splashed into the pond at the far side. I sent *Lisa* for the pintail. She was out a long time swimming, zig zagging across the pond, trying to pick up the scent. I walked around the pond to try and help her. She kept swimming to the edge, coming out a few feet and then going back into the water. I suddenly realised that this was where the fox had been. The scent from the fox was so strong it was overpowering the scent from the duck. The duck certainly wasn't in the water so it must have come out and hidden in the grass. I brought *Lisa* away from the pond about fifty yards and worked her back into the wind. After a few minutes her nose went up and she was off, returning with a duck that was alive and struggling. Better me than the fox, I thought, as I despatched it and put it in my bag.

Walking back I heard that familiar shout from The Greg, *"Fetch your dog!" Lisa* picked up three wigeon and a mallard from the other pond and she was pleased with herself. An enjoyable day! Even the plonker entertained us when he fell in the water. A couple of pints in The Pickerels will go down well tonight.

Sandy didn't fancy the idea of buying another round, so he decided not to join us for our evening visit to see Albert. He kindly allowed us the use of his Mini and I jumped in the drivers seat before The Greg had a chance. It was bad enough being driven by The Greg on a tarmac road, so I didn't like the idea of him testing out his driving skills on the slippery track.

Albert must have seen our headlights coming down the track because when we walked into the bar he was ready for us. There were five pairs of shoes on the bar. Albert said, *"I heard you were a bit low on shoes. Would any of these be of use to you?"* The Greg must have spent his lunch time drinking session informing Albert of my misfortune. Over the years Albert must have told the story a thousand times, about the wildflower who left The Three Pickerels one night and went for a paddle, losing his Hush Puppies in the pond of mud.

While we were in the Pickerels some of the locals came in for a drink. Albert couldn't wait to ask them if they could spare me a pair of shoes. He kept saying it doesn't matter if they are muddy. Leaving The Greg to drink at his own pace I only had a couple of pints that night. I didn't want any more disasters going back to the cabin.

The river ran past The Pickerels and there was a steel ladder fixed to the bank down to the water. I was thinking, if we were to bring a boat, we could get to the cabin and then back to The Pickerels without walking. In another few weeks the track would be too wet to take a car up it. I decided I would try and buy a cheap boat, that was light enough to fit on top of the car, on a roof rack.

I drove back to the cabin without incident and found Sandy asleep in his bunk. We had a fried egg sandwich for our supper and soon after that The Greg lay on his bunk and started to snore. I walked out onto the balcony. It was a beautiful night. Going back in

I put my coat on and poured a good whisky. Taking a chair out onto the balcony I sat and listened to the ducks calling while sipping the whisky and started to think about my children.

The best thing that came out of my first marriage were my four children. Three boys and a girl. Although I was only twenty-one, all I wanted to do was get married and have children. I wanted a boy who I could play football with, and do some of the things that my Father never did with me. After living in digs for three years, I missed the home life with my Mother. In my innocence I thought, that if I was married everything would be like it had been at home. Funny how nothing ever seems to work out the way you think it will. My eldest boy is called David. I gave all the children common names because I didn't want them to suffer the same fate as myself, being the only Vincent in the school.

David was born in 1964, just ten months after we were married. I was so proud of this little fellow I brought my friends in to show him off. The person who stated that, beauty is in the eye of the beholder, certainly hit the nail on the head. They say that there is only one most beautiful baby in the world, and every mother has it. In this case it was the father who had it. Looking back at the photographs we managed to take, between him being sick and messing himself, I now realise how diplomatic my friends must have been when I was showing off my first child. His face had more wrinkles on it than a map of the world, a bald head and to cap it all, he was yellow from jaundice. When you picked him up his first reaction was to throw up all over you. What a little treasure he was! He is now thirty-six and has nearly got out of that habit. He never had any real interest in football, which was just as well, because I was getting to old to play myself.

I introduced him to the shooting scene at a very early age, by allowing him to clean the dog dirt up out of the garden. Well, they were gun dogs! When he was twelve he started to come beating for us with his friend Richard. We still had the shoot at Leverstock Green and shot it every other Saturday in the season. The landlord of a village pub near Dunstable enjoyed the occasional shot, and understood the needs of shooters. Although the pubs were not supposed to open until six, he would let us in through the back door at half past four on a Saturday afternoon. There was always a good log fire burning and we would sit and carry out a post-mortem of the days shooting, with several pints of beer and a plate of sandwiches. Those nearly always present were myself, The Greg,

The Vicar (a nickname for my friend Ian), Tony Wallace and a guest gun. David and Richard were never paid for the beating, but they were allowed as many cans of Coke and bags of crisps that they could manage. Believe me, they certainly took advantage. They were good days and I can still recall the sounds of the laughing.

The following summer I took David to the clay shoot. He was a natural shot and the little bugger beat me with his first go. The first time I took him to the Ouse Washes he was thirteen. I gave him a single barrel twelve bore and he shot a duck with his first shot. When I took him on holiday shooting in Scotland, he was stood next to me, killing wigeon when I couldn't even see them, because it was so dark. It was all too easy for him. He enjoyed it at the time, but it never meant to him what it means to me.

A family man now with two children, and he never shoots. He brings his family to Scotland for a week each year and they stay with us. On an evening we sometimes play scrabble and he beats me. We have the occasional game of golf during the day and he beats me at that as well.

By now I was falling asleep on the chair reminiscing away in my head. I went back into the cabin, took some cotton wool out of my bag and stuffed it in my ears. Sandy saw me and asked if I had any to spare. I have slept in the same room as The Greg before, so I always come prepared.

A lick on the nose woke me and I shone my torch on to my watch. It was ten to five. I could hear the wind outside and it was howling. There was very little wind when I was sitting out there five hours ago. When I went onto the balcony I had to hold on to the rail. The cabin was shaking from the battering the wind was giving it. Thank goodness it's dry, I thought, and with that it started to rain.

I made a cup of tea and lay on my bunk. There was no point going out early this morning, you couldn't see your hand in front of you. After a while I got up and looked at the food rations. I decided to eat one of the ham sandwiches The Greg had thrown in the ration bag. After taking one bite I was nearly sick. Bloody mustard a quarter of an inch thick. Why do people ruin the taste of good food with bloody foul tasting mustard? I swilled my mouth out with my tea to get rid of the disgusting taste, and had some bread and cheese.

An hour later I was heading for the pond with the wind howling around my ears. It was so strong it was blowing *Lisa* sideways as she was walking. If there are any duck about this morning it is going to be interesting. They will either be fighting against the wind and hardly moving, or they will have the wind up their bums and be virtually untouchable.

When I reached the hide I wasn't surprised to find that all of the reeds and grass had blown off the main frame of sticks, which had been pushed into the boggy ground. I had a camouflage net in my bag and tied it on to the sticks pegging the bottom down. The nets are good if they are not blowing about. I have seen people standing in hides that look like shirts blowing about on the washing line, and they wonder why they don't shoot anything.

I heard the whistle and the wings of wigeon going over. Still too dark to see them but, there is nothing better to get the adrenaline going. Someone could see because a shot rang out from the other pond. A couple of minutes later I was in business. A pack of wigeon flew across the pond. I swung the gun so fast I nearly fell out of the hide. It did the trick though, and the bird was down somewhere in the grass. It was still dark so I sent *Lisa*. Two minutes later she was back in the hide pushing the wigeon into my hand. The rain started again and was driving into my face. Wigeon overhead but as I swung the gun the rain blinded me, and I missed. I decided to stand with my back to the pond with the rain driving into the back of my head. It was a good move, I could now see them. I shot two more wigeon before it went quiet. As it became lighter some mallard went over at half the speed of the wigeon, and I missed. I honestly believe I missed in front, which doesn't happen very often. The speed of the earlier wigeon had thrown my judgement. Nearly light and four pintail crossed. I had shot one yesterday and let them go. *Lisa* retrieved the ducks and I went over to The Greg, where she performed again. I think she likes to be the only dog there. It was raining heavy but we enjoyed a good mornings flight, shooting seven wigeon and two mallard between us.

Going to the car to find a dry coat I suddenly realised how slippery the track had become. The rain was still pouring down and the track condition could only get worse. I told The Greg I was going to pack everything in the car and try to get it back to The Pickerels' car park in daylight.

When we arrived on Sunday there was a little wooden shed under the cabin with a chemical toilet in it. During the night the wind had completely removed the shed leaving the chemical toilet sitting there in the open. I don't think it will attract too many callers now.

I don't want to dwell on the subject but I once bought some thermal underwear which was an all-in-one body suit. It was great until I got the call of nature, which in my case was usually at the wrong time. I could have sat on the loo for two hours before I went out and nothing would happen, but sitting in a hide five minutes before the flight was due to start I was usually given two minutes notice to let nature take its course, or else. What a bloody performance I had with this all-in-one body suit. First thing off was the Barbour coat, next roll down waders, then off with the jumper followed with the top half of a boiler suit and shirt, finally peel off and pull down the top half of the all-in-one body suit, then sit there in sub zero temperatures half bloody naked. The cold was such a shock to the system that the usual result was for the bowels to shut up shop and refuse to work. Then the whole process was repeated twenty minutes later. The front fastening on the all-in-one suit was Velcro. Every time it was closed it managed to get a firm grip on my chest hairs. By the end of the week my chest was virtually plucked and oven ready. I even tried cutting a bum flap in the suit but it was too draughty. Eventually it went in the dustbin and I was glad to see the back of it.

The car was packed and we were on our way back along the track. I had a good idea Albert would have his binoculars on us, praying for another disaster to tell everybody about. It was extremely slippery and The Greg had to spend quite a lot of the time outside the car, pushing it sideways, stopping the back end from sliding down the bank. It took the best part of an hour but we made it safely. I am glad we didn't try it in the dark.

Into Greasy Joe's for our breakfast and it was good. The Greg said the ingredients of a good holiday are Greasy Joe's, The Pickerels and duck shooting. He didn't mind which order they came in, as long as they were all in the equation. I had my suspicions that The Pickerels could well have been the most important.

The Greg had been up to The Pickerels in May, when the grazing was being auctioned. He had managed to lease some shooting on one of the washes, which was only half a mile from the gate at the bottom of the track. Unfortunately, there were no ponds on this wash so our plan was to shoot it in January, when it had flooded. We decided to try evening flight on it, rather than walk all the way back to the cabin.

After several games of dominoes and a couple of beers we walked to the wash that The Greg had acquired the shooting rights on. It was basically a large field, three quarters of a mile wide and four hundred yards long. I noticed there were some beasts in the field at the far end, so I suggested we kept away from them. We lined out along the fence next to some small trees and waited for dusk.

Before long the beasts were crossing the field to investigate us, probably hoping for food. As always, the beasts were fascinated with the dog and kept coming close for a sniff, and then leaping back. *Lisa* had seen it all before and virtually ignored them. I shooed them away a number of times but they were persistent and kept returning. I thought the chances of shooting a duck with these beasts leaping about were nil, so I fired a shot to frighten them away.

The result of this was brilliant. They swung around and went into a stampede straight towards Sandy, who was wandering around backwards. Sandy leapt back out of the way and fell over, landing in a fresh warm smelly deposit, which one of the beasts had left on its way over to me. We never shot any ducks that night but I really enjoyed the flight.

Later that night at home, recording the events into my diary, I must admit I had to smile. I never managed to kill Sandy but there was one thing for certain, he won't get the chance to spoil it for me again. I wrote on my list of important things to do. Buy a boat!

CHAPTER 7

Second trip to Pontoon Wash

  During the next few weeks I was studying the 'for sale' advertisements in the local papers, looking for a small boat that I could use to navigate The Hundred Foot River between The Pickerels and Pontoon Wash. I have always liked boats but knew little about them then. When I was a teenager in Hull, I often cycled to Bridlington to go on a fishing trip on a charter boat, catching mainly codling and dabs. The two man crew of the boat provided me with a rod and fresh bait, being nearly always mussels, which they skilfully attached to the hook. If ever I tried to put a mussel on the hook it fell off before the hook was in the water. On the way back to the harbour, one of the crew would steer the boat while the other man gutted the fish that had been caught and threaded string through their gills. I would proudly walk off the boat and along the harbour side carrying a bundle of fish hanging from the string for everyone to see. Sometimes the fish had deteriorated so much on my three hour cycle journey home, that my Mother was suspicious of the fact they might poison us and threw them in the bin.

  Fish was very much a part of our diet. Our next door neighbour worked on the fish docks and three times a week he would give my Mother a large parcel of fish straight from the docks. He must have felt sorry for her trying to rear her brood on next to nothing. He was a bit of a 'do it yourself' man and enjoyed carrying out work on his house. My Father very rarely spoke to him, mocking him because his work was not professional. I think my Father resented his interference. All I can say about it is, the fish was wonderful. My Mother would serve it up on a plate alongside a pile of bread. The fish was so good that the juice ran out of it and we would use the bread to dip into the juice. Unfortunately, the fish sold today in most fish shops is so old it has completely dried up and contains none of the juices which we enjoyed so much.

  I still love fishing being fortunate enough now to live in a good fishing area, with salmon and sea trout on my doorstep and a boat moored up in the harbour just waiting for me to use, when I can find the time.

  We have a tope festival every year and tope are regularly caught in excess of thirty-five pounds. At one time the fish had to be killed and brought ashore to be entered into the competition. It is far better now because the fish are released back into the water alive after a few measurements have been taken. A measurement around the girth and calculated with the length can give a fairly accurate weight of the fish. It is a factor to consider that since this process has been adopted, people are claiming the prize with weights far in excess of any fish that was physically produced at the end of the days fishing. However, these people can't really enjoy their glory if they know they have cheated, and what is most important, the tope population does not suffer.

I spotted a 'for sale' advert offering a ten foot dingy with oars. I knew we would need more than oars to propel the boat against the tide and current on the river but I also knew that Tony Wallace had obtained a small Seagull outboard motor. This was becoming exciting and I couldn't wait to have a look at the boat. I made a telephone call and arranged to view the boat that evening.

It was in a garage when the man showed it to me. A clinker built type boat with lots of copper rivets holding the boards together and it had been varnished. He told me he had renovated the dingy and it looked good. I think I had made my mind up that I was going to buy it before I arrived there. I didn't even try to haggle with the asking price. On to the roof rack it went and I was delighted.

The canal was the nearest water to test the boat and that was twelve miles away. The next Sunday morning me and Ian took it to the canal to carry out the sea trials. Lifting it off the roof rack we carried it to the water's edge. After we had lowered it in the water I asked Ian to hold the bow rope while I went back to the car to fetch the oars. When I returned, Ian had a grin on his face that spread from one side to the other. I looked over the canal bank and was horrified to see the boat was half full of water and sinking fast. The bloody thing was like a colander.

As the stern went down Ian roared with laughing and I couldn't help but join in. Ian said, *"I know the Titanic sank quickly but this is ridiculous."* I was laughing as I held the bow rope helping Ian pull the boat up the canal bank while the water was pouring out of the gaps where the boards overlapped. It was then that I named the boat Titanic as it seemed appropriate.

As I explained earlier, I knew little about boats so I telephoned a friend who sailed. He was amused when I told him what had happened and advised me that while the boat had been out of the water being renovated, the planks of wood it had been constructed with, had dried out and shrunk. He went on to tell me, a clinker built boat has to sit in the water for the planks to soak, causing them to swell, thus sealing the gaps that had allowed the water through that caused the boat to sink.

This was a major problem for me with the nearest water being twelve miles away. If I had left the boat in the canal to soak, I am certain it would be stolen within minutes of me leaving it. Also the boat had been varnished all over which would slow down the soaking process of the planks.

I had a friend who was a first class joiner. He had made several doors and windows for me in the past and he always swore by a waterproof glue called Cascamite. I asked him if the glue would seal the boat if I painted it onto the hull. He said it probably would but it would take several coats to build up enough thickness to seal the gaps between the planks.

I bought three large tins of the glue and set about the task of sealing the boat. The glue comes in a white powder form and by adding water and stirring, it forms a paste. The less water added, the thicker the paste. I meticulously coated the hull with five coats of the glue, pushing plenty into the gaps, until it was apparent that a shell had formed on it. Next Sunday morning we went back to the canal for our second attempt at sea trials. We carefully lifted the boat off the roof rack, carried it to the canal bank and lowered it into the water. It sat there proud in the water with no signs of water sneaking in. Climbing into the boat I rowed Ian up and down the canal for the next hour. The glue had done the job. Wonderful! All we had to do now was borrow Tony's outboard engine and we would have the transport to get from The Pickerels to the cabin on Pontoon Wash and of course, back again for the necessary occasionally refreshments in The Pickerels.

I booked the shooting on Pontoon Wash and we were to go in two weeks time. We were going on the Sunday and shooting Monday, Tuesday and returning after morning flight on Wednesday. I was really looking forward to this trip because there were no plonkers going. We had finally managed to arrange the shooting to coincide with Tony's days off work. There would be me and Tony with Ian and The Greg. The right ingredients for a good laugh and some serious shooting.

I had been telling Ian about The Pickerels and the landlord Albert so he was looking forward to going. I suggested that we could have a run to The Pickerels the following Sunday, Ian could meet Albert and we could try the boat in the river with the outboard engine as a trial run before the shooting trip the following week. If any modifications needed to be carried out we would have a week to do them. Ian agreed and Sunday morning we loaded Titanic on to the roof rack.

One day, during the previous week, I had been over to Letchworth to see Tony and collect the outboard engine. Of course, I wouldn't travel to Tony's without my gun and we had a great day at the pigeon. Tony had asked me to leave *Lisa* at home because he wanted to take his spaniel Grobally, and with him being so young, he might want to play if there was another dog there. Tony had been putting a lot of time into Grobally's training and it would be interesting to see how he was progressing. When I arrived at Tony's house I wasn't surprised to see him at the gate rolling a cigarette. It was a blustery cold day when we set off walking down the track and across the fields. Tony had brought Brady, his black Labrador, as well as Grobally. There would be no chance of Brady wanting to play. He had no interest in playing or shooting. He just came out for the walk to the hide, where he would sleep through until lunch time.

We walked past the field where we had shot pigeons the last time Tony had taken me out. The barley stubble had now been ploughed in. Twenty minutes later we were walking alongside a wide hedge which bordered a huge field sown with rape and the plants were about three inches high. A man stepped out of the hedge carrying a gun. Tony introduced me to this man whose name was George. They then had a conversation about where the pigeon had been feeding that week. After a while Tony told George that we would carry on to the other side of the field and shoot from there. That should keep the pigeons on the move with the shooting at both sides of the field. Shooting from just one side of a large field can create problems. We once planned a day at the pigeons, making the effort to get out early and set out our decoys in the dark. We then settled to wait in a hide we had built the day before. The first pigeons of the day came too early to see the decoys and dropped in at the other side of the field attracting every pigeon to them from a five mile radius. (Best laid plans of mice and men.*)*

Walking around the other side of the field we stopped where there were some large beech trees growing out of the hedgerow. Because we were talking as we walked around the perimeter of the field, we had failed to notice that one of our party was missing. Brady had disappeared. Thinking that he might have been taken ill with a heart attack and rolled into the hedge, Tony walked back the way we had come. When he reached the other side of the field he found Brady fast asleep in the hide next to George. Brady had decided he had gone far enough. He must have thought, why walk to another hide when there is one here. George said, *"As you and Vince set off walking, instead of following you, Brady walked into the hide, turned around three times, laid down and went to sleep."* He had expected Tony to notice Brady was missing and whistle him in. By the time we had reached the other side of the field George realised that we hadn't noticed that Brady was missing so he tried to send Brady to us. He said, *"Brady opened one eye and looked at me. Then he went back to sleep."*

Tony came back with Brady reluctantly following. While he was gone I was busy making a couple of hides between the trunks of the beech trees with some poles and a net I had brought. I set the poles five feet out into the field in an arc and hung the net on them. I then pegged out some rubber decoys which we would replace as soon as possible with dead pigeons. Tony took a catapult out of his bag and fired some weights attached to string over the overhanging bows of the beech trees. He then hoisted some plastic decoys up to make them look like pigeons sitting. Grobally sat and watched the activity with interest while Brady slept. Everything was ready and we climbed into the hides. Grobally walked into the hide and took up position at the back, looking out over the field behind us. Whenever pigeons came from behind, Grobally would wag his tail to let Tony know. It's amazing how he took to it. This was his first time out and he sat there composed like a veteran. I have been out pigeon shooting many times since with Tony and Grobally and the dog always takes up the position of rear lookout. We had a wonderful five hours of shooting with the tree decoys being extremely successful. As usual we ran out of cartridges and collected in the bag. Forty-three pigeon had been shot. Forty went to the game dealer and we ate the other three at a later date, in a pigeon pudding.

On the way back to Tony's house he was talking about Brady. He was telling me that Brady was one of the most obedient dogs he had ever owned but, unfortunately, he had no interest in shooting. One day when returning from pigeon shooting Tony and Brady walked past the village football pitch where the players were preparing for the start of the game. After a few minutes Tony turned around only to see Brady sitting two hundred yards behind him.

Apparently, the referee had blown his whistle for the game to start and Brady thought it was a command to sit.

Later, when Pat had provided her hot home made bread with butter and cheese, I asked Tony why George was there shooting. He explained, that with there being so much ground in the Garden City, the vermin shooting had been divided between the two of them. The hedgerow, where George was shooting, was the boundary between the allocations made to Tony and George. Rather than fall out trying to establish who has the rights to shoot that hedgerow, they both shot it.

Another thick slice and I was on my way home with the outboard in the boot and suffering from indigestion for over indulging with Pat's delicious bread.

It was pleasant driving to Mepal on the Sunday morning with great anticipation of the successful sea trials with Titanic and the outboard motor, and as always, when Ian was there we had plenty of laughs. We arrived at The Pickerels at ten past twelve with Titanic on the roof rack. Going into The Pickerels I introduced Ian to Albert who told Ian he was always pleased to meet wildflowers and the crack flowed from there. The usual Sunday morning domino school were in there dressed in their winter woollies. Ian continued to entertain for an hour, drinking four pints of beer to my two. I managed to persuade him to leave the bar by telling him, once we have launched Titanic he can go back in and I would take the boat up the river for the trials with the outboard attached.

Going outside we untied the ropes that were securing the boat onto the roof rack. The wind had picked up and I was concerned that the boat would be caught by the wind and blow out of our hands. I told Ian to take a firm grip and to lift when I shouted. I got hold of my end and shouted for Ian to lift. We had lifted it over the edge of the roof rack and away from the car when the luck of the Raw struck, and it all went wrong. Ian stepped back and stumbled. The boat seemed to spin out of our hands landing on the car park tarmac upside down with its little keel in the air. I couldn't believe what I was seeing. Titanic had given birth! When the boat hit the ground the shell that had been formed with the glue had come loose and it was just sitting there loosely on the boats hull as though it was having a piggy back. I stood there speechless. Turning my head my worst fears were confirmed. There was Albert and the domino school standing at The Pickerels window laughing so much they were in tears. There was nothing we could do except put the boat back on the roof rack and have another pint, much to the delight of our audience.

I spent every evening the following week painting a new glue shell onto the boat ready for our trip the following Sunday. As I was working on the boat I tried to encourage *Lisa* to sit in it. She had far more sense than me and approached Titanic with extreme caution, refusing to have anything to do with it. The thought of the wigeon flighting and the pure peace of Pontoon Wash kept me busy. The boat should be so useful. Apart from guns and cartridges, we had to carry enough provisions of food and water, with plenty of spare clothing, two and a half miles up a very muddy track, and they can get extremely heavy. I have seen men setting off up the track, full of enthusiasm and fully loaded with equipment. Every so often they jettison a bag or a water container with the intention of coming back for it. Little bundles where positioned about every five hundred yards up the track on the way to the cabin and were collected later.

Sunday morning and the excitement was mounting while loading the car. *Lisa* was keeping very close to me to make sure she wouldn't be left behind. Sally, the young black Labrador, had never been wildfowling and couldn't understand what all the fuss was about. I might give her a day out at the end of the season, I thought, depending how she responds to the continuing training.

Ian's wife, Irene, drove him to my house and between them they emptied the contents of the car onto the pavement. I suggested that she didn't drive off immediately because we were going to have to thin out Ian's luggage. There were three suitcases, a couple of large plastic bags, five carrier bags of food, a five gallon container full of water, a suit on its hanger in a polythene bag and a litre bottle of whisky. I picked up the whisky and told her to take the rest away. We eventually loaded some of his luggage into my car after discarding one of the suitcases, one of the big bags, the container of water and the suit.

The Greg was taking Tony and we met up with them in a car park in Baldock. Grobally was in the back of The Greg's car making a nuisance of himself. He was so used to being in Tony's jeep where he would sit on the front seat, he didn't think much of being put in the back. When I was a passenger in Tony's jeep, Grobally would push himself between Tony and myself and sit there looking ahead, as though he was driving. If you tried to push him out of the way he would give you a filthy look as much as to say, who do you think you are pushing. Apparently, he had climbed between The Greg and Tony and inadvertently knocked the car out of gear a couple of times. This wouldn't do the engine any good as The Greg always drives with the accelerator hard down on the floor. Tony was getting cross with Grobally and after several warnings he decided to sort Grobally out. He climbed out of the front door of the car and opened the back door where Grobally was sitting. This young dog who had pushed his luck too far, knew he was in trouble. He realised he was about to receive a clip around the ear so he played his ace. He started yelling with the most horrendous noise before Tony got near him. You would have thought he was being murdered. The only way Tony could shut him up was to stroke him. Not the thing that was intended. This was Grobally's defence method and he used it whenever he was in trouble and he had an audience. Tony said if nobody was around, Grobally just took his punishment quietly.

Off we went again with my car in front and Titanic wobbling about on the roof rack. The Greg was behind about six inches from my bumper. I was pleased when we arrived without any incidents.

Extremely carefully and totally sober we lifted Titanic off the roof rack. We then carried it into the field and across to the bank of The Hundred Foot River where we lowered it into the water. Ian held the bow rope while the rest of us unloaded the vehicles and stacked the luggage on the bank. I was thinking a ten foot dingy is not going to be adequate for all this equipment. A barge would have been more useful. I climbed into the boat and they passed down the luggage. Carefully stacking it, I made use of the limited space. After packing most of the luggage into the boat The Greg and Tony said they would carry the rest, including the guns. The next thing to do was to fit the outboard. I had started the engine several times during the week in a barrel of water and it always started first pull. I fastened it on the stern and Ian climbed onto the bow while Tony held the rope. The Greg had *Lisa* on a lead and she had a worried look on her face. After switching the petrol on and setting the choke I pulled the cord expecting the engine to roar into life, but all it did was splutter. Fifty pulls later the bloody thing was still spluttering. I had used up more energy than I would have done if I had walked down to the cabin carrying all the luggage. I was still pulling the cord as The Greg was suggesting that we could drag the boat along, like they did with the African Queen, when suddenly the engine burst into life. The river was in spate running down to The Wash which was the direction we were heading and we launched off going with it. After a couple of minutes, I looked back and could see The Greg and Tony in the distance. *Lisa* was standing on her hind legs looking at me.

After all the planning it had worked. We were moving fast and in no time we were going past Willow Wash. On we went and it wasn't long before we saw the cabin on Pontoon Wash. As we approached I steered the boat into a part of the bank that was low and cut the engine. Titanic glided into the bank and Ian jumped off the boat and secured the bow rope to a bush. I was really pleased. That was far better than walking and I couldn't believe how quickly we had got there. I suggested that we should unload the luggage onto the bank and while Ian was carrying it into the cabin I would go back for the boys who were walking. I passed the luggage to Ian and he stacked it on the bank. I told him to hang onto the bow rope until I started the engine and then let go. After another hundred and forty pulls, the engine screamed. That was when the luck of the Raw struck again. Instead of Ian letting go of the rope, he decided to give the boat a bloody big push away from the bank. With the big push being against the direction that the screaming engine was trying to propel the boat, the results were disastrous. The bow of the boat lifted out of the water and to my horror it kept coming up. I couldn't believe it. In no time at all it was almost vertical and Titanic was going down again. As the bow came up I stood up, and that is how I went under with my ship, offering a salute to Ian at the last second.

I wouldn't recommend swimming in the river in January fully clothed, donning a pair of waders. When I surfaced I saw the boat was upside down and going down the river with the flow. I couldn't let it go, Tony's engine was still hanging on it. I swam after it and managed to grab the rope. The hardest part was swimming to the side towing the boat with the river wanting to take me and Titanic on to The Wash. Reaching the side, exhausted, I passed the rope to Ian who was trying not to laugh. He tied the boat to a lump of drift wood and helped me out. I stood on the bank shivering and not believing what had happened, when a shout from Ian alerted me to the fact that the knot he had tied in the rope had come undone and Titanic was off again heading to The Wash. If it hadn't been for Tony's engine I would have let it go.

I ran along the river bank, which wasn't easy with waders full of water. When I was in front of the boat I dived in and swam to it. Once again I fought with the current to get to the side and Ian

I went under with my ship offering a salute.

helped me out. He tried not to laugh but when I grinned he couldn't hold it back any longer. It all came out in a roar of laughter you would have heard a mile away. I was helping Ian to pull the boat out when he asked me if I would like another dip as the oars where somewhere in the river. I told him they could stay there. Ian said, *"You need a drink!"* and ran towards the cabin. I was slowly trudging towards the cabin shivering when Ian came towards me with a glass of whisky. I held my hand out for it but instead of giving it to me he held it back and said, *"I rescued you, I should have it."* With that, he swallowed the contents.

I was dried and changed and had hung the engine on the balcony rail by the time The Greg and Tony arrived. They knew something had happened to me by the grin on Ian's face. The only saving grace was, we were too far away from The Pickerels for Albert to fix his binoculars on me. *Lisa* gave me that look that meant, it serves you right, and then decided to check out the smells in the cabin to find out if any other dogs had been in recently.

The Greg and Ian paid the compulsory visit to The Pickerels that night on foot. I spent the night desperately trying to dry my waders and shooting jacket with the use of the oven and enjoyed a couple of drams with Tony in the cabin discussing dogs. Grobally wasn't sure what was going on but he knew it was an adventure because his tail never stopped wagging.

We could hear Ian and The Greg returning from their pilgrimage to Albert's when they were a quarter of a mile away. Ian has a distinctive laugh and seems to see the funny side of everything. They had promised earlier that they wouldn't tell Albert about my sinking but I didn't believe them.

Up the steps they came and into the cabin. Ian rummaged in one of his carrier bags and came out with a big parcel. As he unwrapped it I could see it was a great slab of bread pudding. The Greg roared with laughter and said, *"No wonder the bloody boat sunk. It had three ton of bread pudding in it."* Grobally fixed his eyes on the slab and started drooling. Ian tore a lump off, which was the size of his fist, and offered it to Grobally, who grabbed it nearly removing Ian's hand at the same time. No more than two chews and he had swallowed it, much to our amusement. You could see the shape of the lump of pudding going down the dog's throat. A good swallow and he was ready for more and Ian was willing to oblige. After Grobally had eaten a third of the slab, Ian put it away in the bag. There was a look of disappointment on Grobally's face. He would have been quite happy to have scoffed the lot.

Another dram and we were ready for some sleep. I must have been a bit slow because the boys took the three bottom bunks and I was left with a top one, much to *Lisa's* disgust. We were amused when Ian put on his pyjamas. We usually just slip off our trousers and jumper and dive straight into our sleeping bags. The cabin was warm with the oven being on, so I opened the sleeping bag and laid it loosely on top of me.

If I need to rise early in a morning I usually wake up several times during the night, in between dreams, to check the time. I have heard people say that you only actually dream for a few seconds. I can assure you I dream all night and they are always disasters. In my dreams I have been killed in more ways than most stunt men. I have been shot, stabbed, strangled, drowned, hung, garrotted, driven over cliffs, been eaten by crocodiles and run over by a train, just to name a few.

I eventually went to sleep and my dream started. This dream was a real disaster. I dreamt that I had woken up in the cabin and it was daylight. The boys had gone out for morning flight and I had been left behind. My immediate reaction was to jump out of bed as quickly as possible. Unfortunately, I was still asleep and in my dream I didn't realise I was in the top bunk. I jumped out of bed and soon woke up as I hit the floor in a great heap which brought a yell out of me. Within seconds I had two dogs leaping all over me and three torches shining on me. It was half past two in the morning and the cabin was shaking from the roars of laughing from the boys. I nonchalantly climbed back into my bunk nursing a few bruises and decided to stay awake. I inserted fresh cotton wool into my ears to avoid the full decibels of The Greg's snoring. The cotton wool I had inserted earlier had shot out of my ears when I hit the floor and Grobally had eaten it.

Being the first to rise I put the kettle on the gas ring and went out onto the balcony for some fresh air. The cabin smelt of stale booze, cigarettes, and sweaty socks with a hint of drying Barbour coat and waders. It was pitch black out there and I could hear the owls calling to each other. I started to think of the wigeon and became quite excited. Although we were only two and a half miles from the road it seemed like total isolation. The only sounds to be heard were wildlife calling. No car horns or screaming lorry engines. This was pure peace and I loved it.

Going back into the cabin, I poured the tea. The boys had woken up and The Greg was having a good scratch. Ian said he had been bitten by a flea. The Greg suggested that Ian should look in his sleeping bag. He said, *"If a flea had swallowed any of Ian's blood it will be laid on its back, pissed."* We drank the tea and got ready. The Barbour coat and waders were reasonably dry and I was pleased I had stayed in the cabin to organise the drying, instead of going to The Pickerels. I had hung the waders up from the ceiling so the heat from the oven went up the legs and the coat over a chair which I placed in front of the oven. I would imagine this little Calor gas oven has dried more clothes than it has cooked dinners.

Tony had never been there before so I told him to stay with me and we headed to the pond at the far end of Pontoon Wash. The Greg took Ian to a pond near the middle. There was a stiff breeze blowing and it was dry. The last time I was there the rain was horizontal. We were making our way across the wash and I was becoming excited. Two men, with their dogs at heel, heading off to try their luck. Most people will just be getting out of their beds with the prospect of another boring day at work. I remember thinking, what a pleasure it was just to be there, regardless of the bag.

Arriving at the pond, we made a couple of hides about thirty yards apart. Settling in my hide I waited in anticipation, loving every minute of it. *Lisa* pushed up against me and gave me an affectionate look. We were both ready and we didn't have to wait long. The whistle and wing beat of wigeon right over the top, but too dark to see them. Another pack of wigeon and still too dark. It seemed to be taking for ever for day to break. I thought I heard geese a long way away but decided I must be hearing things. I was beginning to think that all the ducks will have flighted by the time day breaks. A glimmer of light and a bunch of teal flew across the pond with such speed I never got the gun to my shoulder. Two shots rang out from Tony and two splashes into the pond. I heard a whimper from Grobally, followed by a stern voice telling him to stay. *Lisa's* tail wagged and a pack of wigeon came from behind, low over my head. I took a right and left. It was like down the line shooting. Moments later and more wigeon and we were both shooting at them which resulted in three splashes. I could hear the guns on the other pond and they were having as much shooting as us, if not more. As it became light half a dozen mallard flew over very high. I decided they were too high for me but Tony killed one stone dead. Tony is an extremely good shot and I am quite happy to leave the high birds for him.

As soon as it was full daylight the ducks that were still flighting were too high to shoot at. We waited an hour without another shot being fired. It was pleasant enough sitting there but hunger was starting to bite. We walked to the other pond and the two dogs shared the picking up. An enjoyable morning flight shooting fifteen ducks between us.

Back in the cabin I cooked the breakfast. Egg, bacon and beans. Not quite the standard of Greasy Joe's but not too bad. We discussed the flight over our meal and it turned out that The Greg had heard the geese also. What a bonus it would be to have geese over us as well as the ducks.

By the time we had drunk another cup of tea and finished the washing up, it was eleven. I stood on the balcony looking over the wash. There was the odd pack of wigeon flighting down the centre of the washes like dots in the sky. It would have been pleasant sat out there by a pond but there would be nothing to shoot at. I wanted to strip the outboard engine and give it a good clean after it's dunking. Tony stayed with me and The Greg and Ian decided that a hair of the dog in The Pickerels would be a good idea and set off once again along the muddy track.

I had brought a small tool kit with me including adjustable spanner, plug spanner and a few screw drivers. We lifted the engine off the handrail and emptied the tank of petrol and water into the grass. Taking the engine inside the cabin, we stripped it down and dried every bit. By half past one it was back together and hanging on the handrail outside with fresh petrol in the tank. We needed to know if it would work, so I gave it a pull. It burst into life immediately. I stopped it before any damage was caused. Going over to the river bank we inspected Titanic. Considering what it had been through it looked remarkably well with the glue skin still intact. We decided to put the boat in the water and fit the engine to it. Carefully we lowered the boat in and I climbed into it. *Lisa* turned away as though she was too frightened to look. Tony passed down the engine and I put it on the stern. With the weight of me and the engine at the stern, the bow was well clear of the water. I realised then that the bow needed some ballast to counter the weight. Tony climbed down into the bow and the boat sat nicely balanced. I tried to start the engine. After pulling the cord for fifteen minutes, all I could get was a splutter or two. Tony tried with the same results. Back to the drawing board or in this case, the balcony handrail. We took the engine off and carried it back to the cabin, fitting it on the hand rail. Tony went into the cabin to fetch the tools. While he was in there I gave the engine another pull and it burst into life again. I quickly turned it off. We decided that there must have been a bit of dirt on the plug and carrying the engine back from the boat to the cabin it had been dislodged. Back to the boat we went with the engine and fixed it into position. With Tony in the bow as ballast, I pulled the engine rope. Not a bloody splutter. After another fifteen minutes of pulling the rope I was exhausted. The luck of the Raw! We have found the only outboard engine in history that doesn't like water. Hang the bloody thing on the fence in the dry and it goes first time. Not being the sort of sensible fellow who knows when he is beaten, I kept on pulling at it. I think it must have realised I wasn't going to give in because after half an hour it reluctantly started. We had twenty minutes in the boat up and down the river, with the dogs running parallel along the river bank. The engine ran well, although it did struggle against the tide. Steering into the side I turned the engine off. I tried to start it again immediately and it refused. It took another ten minutes of vigorous pulling before it started again.

Walking back to the cabin for a cup of tea, I could see the figures of The Greg and Ian coming along the track about a mile away. We had a couple of sandwiches with our tea and stole a slice of the bread pudding before Ian arrived. I could understand why Grobally liked it, although I needed to chew it for a bit longer than the dog did.

The Greg and Ian arrived at the cabin laughing and joking and I had some tea ready for them. They were saying a salesman had come into The Pickerels while they were there and tried to sell Albert an ice machine. They said it was so cold in there that the salesman took his gloves out of his pocket and put them on while he was talking to Albert. The Greg had told the salesman he would stand a better chance of obtaining a sale if he was selling electric fires. After The Greg had told us this story him and Ian roared with laughter again. They really enjoyed their trips to see Albert.

It was time to get ready for evening flight. The wind was the same as this morning but the sky was thickening with clouds. Me and Tony went back to the far pond and took up position to wait. I saw the others wander out a little later and head for another pond. Just before dusk everything seems to go still. There were little birds flying into the bushes around the pond jostling for a sheltered position to roost. I thought, if we were lucky enough to fire a few shots they will be looking for somewhere quieter to spend the night. A harrier started to hunt in the middle of the wash dipping down within seconds. Another vole bites the dust! The silence was broken by two shots from the other pond. I heard a little whine of excitement from Grobally who was quickly told to be quiet. Three pintail crossed the other side of the pond and Tony took one out. Seconds later a dozen mallard and we had one each. It's as though someone waves a flag at a certain time and the ducks all come together. A bunch of teal and Tony scored twice. A few minutes later there were more wigeon and I managed one as they swung low over the pond. I heard the geese again and I knew from their calls they were greylags. Half an hour later and it was dark. The flight was over. The dogs collected the ducks and we walked to the other pond. The Greg and Ian had two teal which we let Grobally pick, much to the disappointment of *Lisa*.

Our dinner was corned beef out of a tin with beans and eggs, with dessert being a lump of Ian's bread pudding. Sitting at the little table for an hour we discussed the shooting. The Greg had heard the geese as I did and he seemed to think it was a small skein a good half mile away. Ian washed up and I tied the ducks to the balcony rail to keep them cool. The Greg wanted to go back to The Pickerels and asked if we wanted to go with him. We couldn't all go together as the cabin didn't lock and some opportunist could lift four guns while we were enjoying ourselves. Tony insisted on staying. I fancied going in Titanic if the bloody engine would start. That was the plan sorted. Three of us would go in Titanic.

She was moored about forty yards down from the cabin tied to a strong bush. We climbed into the boat with me at the stern, The Greg at the bow and Ian in the middle. I would say that was her limit. One more body would have sunk her. The river was still running quite fast down to The Wash in the opposite direction to which we had to go. The Greg untied her and hung onto the bush until I started the engine. After what seemed like ten minutes, it started and The Greg pushed the bow away from the bank. We were underway but not very fast. The engine was working hard trying to push the combined weight of the three of us against the flow of the river. After a few minutes we were going past the cabin. Tony was at the window with a roll up in his mouth and he gave us a wave. The Greg had his torch on so I could see where to steer. After about ten minutes the engine decided to cut out and we soon started off back in the direction we had come from. Tony was smiling as we passed the cabin in the opposite direction while I was pulling the engine rope and pleading with it to start. When we had drifted past where the boat had been moored, the engine burst into life again and once again we passed the cabin and the smiling Tony, who had trouble keeping his cigarette in his mouth because he was laughing so much.

This time the engine kept going and half a mile from The Pickerels the illuminated sign on the pub wall flashed on and off three times. Albert must have seen the light coming up the river and he was signalling to us. He never missed a trick! We eventually pulled up alongside the steel ladder on the bank by the pub wall and tied the boat to it. It took Titanic three quarters of an hour against the flow of the river. At least it will be a lot quicker going back, I thought, when the flow will be going with us.

Tony laughing as we passed the cabin window in Titanic.

I was right not to believe The Greg and Ian when they said they wouldn't tell Albert about my misfortune in the water. When we walked in the bar Albert couldn't wait to offer me a pair of swimming trunks and a snorkel. It was a normal sort of night in there, freezing cold but fun. At nine-thirty a woman and two men came in for half an hour and talked to Albert. After they had gone Albert told us they were on the committee of the parish council and had just come from the meeting. We noticed they had left a book behind and when Albert wasn't looking we peeped in it. It was the minute book from their meetings. For the sake of reprisals, I'm not saying who, but one of us made an entry in the book that could be classed as suggestive. It referred to a relationship between the chairman and the local vicar's wife. I would love to have seen their faces when the minutes of the previous meeting were read out at the next meeting.

Time to go and a little lecture to my crew before they climbed into the boat, along the lines of, don't do anything stupid and sit still. I climbed into the boat and for once the engine started relatively easy. The trouble was the luck of the Raw had struck and the tide was running in fast. That meant the poor little engine had to fight against the tide all the way back to the cabin. We arrived back safely, three quarters of an hour later, with enough petrol to spare to fill a cigarette lighter and dragged the boat out of the river.

It was still windy with odd breaks in the cloud when I last looked out on the balcony. That was before I climbed into my bunk at twelve. At two I woke up by the call of nature. Climbing down quietly I went out onto the balcony to water the grass below. What a wonderful sight outside. The dark cloud had all been replaced with white fleecy cloud and the moon was up and bright. I stood there and watched for a few minutes. There were wigeon flighting past so close I could have shot them from the balcony. Going back in I woke the boys and told them the wigeon were flighting under the moon and I was going out. The Greg accused me of dreaming again and asked me to check. I told him there was no need to check, they were definitely there. A few minutes later we were all going down the cabin steps and lining out along Pontoon Wash with the wigeon whistling over us. The wash had started to flood and there was about three inches of water on it. The wigeon were flying low over the water and then swinging up in front of us like teal. The shooting was brilliant and went on for two hours. The water was getting deeper and *Lisa* was picking the wigeon up before they drifted away on the water with the wind blowing them. I could see further down the wash that Grobally was busy too. I don't know how many cartridges I fired but I suddenly realised I had ran out when the luck of the Raw struck again. The greylag geese were out in front. They were very quiet but you could clearly see them in the sky passing between me and The Greg I stood and admired them as The Greg took one out. I had hung my bag on a small tree and as *Lisa* was bringing back the wigeon I was putting them in the bag. I walked back to the cabin with the goose and my heavy bag. Me and The Greg had shot eighteen wigeon between us. Deciding that was enough for one flight, I sat on the balcony watching. The boys shot a couple more and then came in to the cabin. We were all excited at what we had witnessed. A pure fluke. If it hadn't been for the call of nature we would have slept through it all. I learnt a lot from that day about checking the weather and the moon, not to mention the tides.

A couple of hours sleep and up again for morning flight. The moon had gone down and it was quite dark. I noticed the water had risen to six inches deep. The ponds had filled up and disappeared under the flood. Lining out along the path I had used to get to the far pond we used small trees as cover. The ducks must have worn themselves out through the night because they didn't appear. As light broke Tony shot a mallard and that was it. Walking back for breakfast I felt sorry for the voles which were desperately swimming from one tuft of grass to the other trying to stay out of the water. Grobally received a clip around the ear for eating a couple of voles when he thought Tony wasn't watching. A variation of diet from the bread pudding which he had been scrounging for the last couple of days.

After breakfast and the washing up finished, we laid on the bunks feeling rather knackered. It wasn't long before The Greg was asleep and snoring, causing another distribution of cotton wool. We slept until three in the afternoon and I felt better for it. When we went out for evening flight the water was still rising. A small area of land around the cabin was higher than the wash and was still dry, although there were some very boggy bits in it where you could sink to your waist. A vast number of voles had taken refuge on it. I had never seen so many voles in my life. You would have thought the Pied Piper of Hamelin had just walked by. The way the water was rising they were all going to die by tomorrow night unless they cross the little bridge to the bank of The Hundred Foot River. I suppose it is natures control over the vole population. Some will find the bridge and survive to breed while others will perish.

We lined out again and I had to try and find a place that was shallow because *Lisa's* legs were not very long and the water was continually rising. The wind had picked up in strength and the water was lapping up my waders. As light was fading a massive pack of wigeon filled the sky. There were eight barrels fired with four wigeon coming down. I heard the geese again and strained my eyes to see them. They came from behind me about fifty yards to my right. I was tempted to shoot but resisted the temptation. They flew safely on without realising their potential danger.

After scraping up the last of the beans and sausages we had them for tea. It was our last night and The Greg was missing Albert. Tony was happy to stay behind with the dogs so the three intrepid piss artists risked the voyage again in Titanic. We filled the tank with petrol and took the can with us in case the engine needed more. Although we still had the flow against us going and the tide against us coming back, the little boat coped pretty well, when I could get the engine started.

We had a good night in The Pickerels listening to Albert's stories and playing dominoes. The Greg and Ian were in good form and probably drank far more than they should have done. After much laughing and giggling in the boat I got them safely back to the cabin.

The Greg walked in and immediately poured himself a large gin. We spent the next hour drinking and reminiscing about life and previous experiences. Grobally finished off the bread pudding and went to sleep. The Greg was swallowing the gin as though it was going out of fashion and his eyes were pink. After the bottle was empty he asked if anybody had any food left as the booze always made him feel hungry. There were only a few eggs left and they had been allocated for breakfast in the morning. The Greg was disappointed but his face lit up when I found, in the bottom of my bag, some stale cheese sandwiches which I had forgotten to eat in the car when I was travelling the previous Sunday. I told him they were old and stale but that didn't deter him. *"I will fry them,"* he said, and placed them in the frying pan. When they were ready he lifted them out of the pan and they were dripping with fat. *"Lovely grub!"* said The Greg, and to my amazement he scoffed the lot. A quarter of an hour later he climbed into his sleeping bag looking contented. After ten minutes of grunting and breaking wind he suddenly sat up and said *"I think I am going to be sick!"* I am not surprised I thought as I watched him head for the cabin door. He never had time to put his boots on and ran out of the door in his long white socks. I could hear him running down the steps at the side of the cabin. Five minutes later he returned and said, *"That's better."* He must have stepped into one of the boggy holes outside because there was no sign of his long white socks any more. There was just pure slimy mud up both legs to four inches above his knees. He just strolled back to his bunk and slid into his sleeping bag with muddy socks still on and he was snoring in two minutes

Ian went to sleep and me and Tony sat on the balcony and watched the moon come up. It was a similar night to the previous one and there were plenty of wigeon flighting. Tony is like myself and didn't feel the need to shoot any more on this trip. The water was too deep now for the dogs to work properly and we were more than pleased with our efforts. A lot had been learnt from our mistakes. After watching the wigeon for an hour and a fly past from the greylags, we retired to our bunks.

The next morning the water was two feet deep over the washes and three inches deep under the cabin. Not a sign of the voles. The harriers and owls will now have to hunt elsewhere. We packed our things and headed home. For once the tide was with us and Titanic was extremely useful ferrying wildfowlers and equipment to The Pickerels car park. We did learn something of importance. If we were going to shoot the washes after they have flooded we would need a suitable flat bottomed boat with a hull that, while floating, would slide over barbed wire fences without being damaged.

We were just working lads struggling to pay the mortgage and raise a family. We couldn't afford the luxury of new boats. Me and Tony had several more trips to the washes when they were flooded in a few different craft we had managed to obtain and convert for the job, which resulted in some exciting shooting and the usual disasters for the Raw but that's another story to tell one day.

CHAPTER 8

A trip to the Solway Firth

Stan was looking for someone to join himself and his friend, Frank, on a trip to shoot on the Solway Firth East of Dumfries in Scotland. After he had mentioned it to me he didn't need to look any further. A quick phone call to The Vicar, a nickname for my friend Ian, and that was the party of four. Stan said he would arrange accommodation in a guest house for the second week in January. My daughter Jacky's birthday falls on the 11th of January and I would like to apologise to her now that I was always away shooting when her birthday fell. Better family planning would have ensured that the children's birthdays occurred in the closed season.

Stan wanted to take his Morris Minor van to Scotland because he had arranged to pick up some parts for one of his old bangers. He had about twenty old cars which he called 'collectable'. To me, they were a load of rusty junk, which he kept in his orchard and they deteriorated quicker than he could carry out any renovation work. He didn't seem to mind if they rusted away and fell to bits. What mattered to Stan was, that he had managed to obtain them and they belonged to him and nobody else. I have been unfortunate enough in the past to have endured several journeys in the Morris Minor van. The passenger side window was stuck, in the open position, with the glass being one inch from the top. I don't know whether the drivers side window was stuck or not but Stan always had it half way down, regardless of the weather. There was no wonder that he always had a dewdrop hanging off the end of his nose. Stan said that he knew Frank well and he would take him in the van if me and Ian could make our own way there. Poor Frank can't have known the van very well or he would have declined the offer and walked.

Ian had a fairly new Cortina and I was to travel with him. I had read about the Solway Firth and therefore knew that there were a lot of geese there in January. This of course can mean that there will be a lot of wildfowlers there also. What a strange breed the wildfowler is! Fifty percent of them are caring intelligent people who respect other people and their quarry. The other fifty percent are loud, rude, ignorant, greedy and don't give a monkey's for anybody except themselves. I have seen them shooting at birds, a hundred yards away, ruining the chance of success for the wildfowler that the birds were about to fly over.

The Vicar was always good fun to travel with and I was looking forward to the journey. Another adventure into new territory. I wondered what was in store for us. The weather was typical January, cold, windy with occasional snow. Sunday morning we loaded up the car with our equipment and I reluctantly left my hide behind because of the lack of space. It was a case of the hide or the dog. You can always make some form of a hide but you can't make a dog like my *Lisa*. Consequently, the hide was put back in the garage.

I was thinking what the guest house would be like where we were going to stay for a week. Stan had booked it from an advert in a magazine. I prefer to know where I am staying but you can't go three hundred miles to Scotland just to see the accommodation before you book it.

Nine in the morning we met up with Stan and Frank at the M1 junction. We said we would follow the van up the motorway and it wasn't long before we regretted that decision. After a couple of hours we had only travelled eighty miles. Stan pulled into a service station and we followed. Me and Ian sat in the car and watched Stan and Frank get out of the van. Frank's face was blue with cold. He stood there stamping his feet and waving his arms around trying to create some circulation. He must have been an Arsenal Football Club supporter because he had most of the kit on, including hat, scarf and jersey. Stan had a woolly hat pulled down over his forehead. His eyes were running and his usual dewdrop was in place. He was totally obsessed with fresh air. I am convinced that one day he will climb out of the van and drop dead with pneumonia. Me and Ian got out of the car. Ian went over to Frank to console him. *"Never mind the cold Frank, we are nearly a quarter of the way there. At this rate we should arrive sometime tomorrow."* Frank asked if he could come in the back of the car for the rest of the journey and put the dog in the van. *"Sorry Frank,"* I said, *"I'm not putting my dog in that van. She will freeze to death and I might need her to retrieve some geese."* *"What about me?"* said Frank. I told him I didn't know he retrieved, but if he brought some geese back to me this week, he could come home in the back of the car. Frank couldn't see the funny side of my remarks and followed Stan into the restaurant for some hot coffee.

We sat at the table in the restaurant drinking coffee and watching Frank thaw out. Stan was quite happy to be cold. He always stated that the cold weather is healthy because it kills off all the germs. He was certainly a character, totally obsessed with collecting old cars and guns. He was more excited about the fact that he was going to pick up a second hand door for one of his old cars than he was about the prospect of getting under the geese on the Solway Firth.

I remember going with him to buy an old car. I took him in my car so he could drive the new rust heap back home to carry out its final rotting in the scrap yard he called his orchard. We travelled the best part of two hundred miles to find this car that had been advertised in the Exchange & Mart. Stan calls this publication his Bible. We found the house and knocked on the door. A man who looked just as weird as Stan greeted us and took us to his garage at the bottom of his drive. He lifted up the garage door and there was the car. It turned out to be an old Jaguar. I was thinking that the condition of this car was far too good for Stan to buy. There wasn't any rust on it! Stan looked around the car with great interest. He would never have made a poker player. You could see from his face that he just had to own this car. He said to the man, *"I see from your advert you want fifteen hundred pounds for it."* The man nodded his head and said, *"That is correct."* Stan said, *"I will give you a thousand for it!"* The man never said a word or showed any emotion. He just calmly closed the garage door and walked back into his house leaving us standing there. We looked at each other and I started to laugh. Stan didn't laugh. He looked a worried man. *"I have got to have that car!"* he said. I told him it was too good to put in his scrap yard as it would show all the others up. Stan told me he was going to rent a lock up garage to put this one into, if the man would sell it to him. I suggested that he made the man a sensible offer. We went back to the house door and knocked again. The man came to the door and stood there. Stan said to him. *"I will give you twelve hundred!"* The man turned around and closed the door again. Stan knocked on the door again and the man returned. Before Stan had a chance to speak the man said. *"Either give me fifteen hundred or clear off."* Stan said, *"It's a deal,"* and shook the man's hand. When we arrived back at Stan's house I asked him where he had learnt the skills to negotiate like that. Stan told me it didn't matter because he could sell the car for two thousand pounds the next day.

He was kidding himself. He would never sell it. It was now part of the collection and it will stay there until it rots away.

We were on the M6 again heading for Scotland. Frank had wrapped his football scarf around his face, wrapped two blankets around his legs and found himself a pair of fleecy lined mittens for the rest of the journey in the mobile freezer. Driving over Shap, the Cumbria hills looked beautiful, covered in snow with the sun glistening down on them. There were only two lanes clear for traffic. The fast lane was under a foot of snow.

It was dark when we eventually arrived and we soon found the Guest House. It was only a short way from a watering hole, so that was a bonus. I rang the bell and the door was opened by a tall upright man. He had a neatly trimmed moustache, standing there with his arms by his sides and his chest sticking out, he looked like a sentry on guard. He spoke with a strong Scottish accent, which I can only describe as abrupt. *"You will be the shooting party, follow me!"* He turned around and marched up the hall with his arms swinging by his sides. Stopping halfway down the hall outside a cupboard he said, *"This cupboard is for your coats, hats, scarves and boots. I don't want those kind of garments in the bedrooms!"* He then marched on and took us into the sitting room where he commanded us to sit and proceeded to give us a lecture that went something like- *"I am a retired Sergeant Major and I will not tolerate any nonsense from wildfowlers or anybody else. Any trouble and you will answer to me!"* Ian said that it was very kind of him to let us know and asked what time dinner was. The man didn't even realise that Ian was being sarcastic and said, *"In one hour and don't be late. I will show you to your rooms!"*

What a bundle of fun we had found here! The rooms were basic but looked clean. There were two beds in each room so I went in with Ian while Frank and Stan had the other room. I told Ian that I was going back downstairs to see Field Marshall Montgomery, to find out where *Lisa* was going to sleep as kennels had been mentioned in the advert. Ian laughed and said that he liked the name but he thought we should shorten it to Monty. I went downstairs and found Monty standing to attention at the kitchen door. I tentatively asked him about a kennel for my dog. He took a deep breath and said. *"Fetch your dog in and I will show you to its quarters. I will provide you with its dinner and you will feed it before you have your dinner!"* I told him I had brought food for my dog and her name was *Lisa*. He carried on talking in the same tone. *"I always provide food for the dogs that stay here. Now go and fetch her!"* I couldn't believe that I was on my way as instructed. When I returned with *Lisa* I was almost tempted to salute. Following him out through a back door we were in an illuminated yard. There were two kennels. Give this man his due, he might be a pain in the backside and his house is very basic, but the kennels were brilliant. There was a good sized run which was spotless. The sleeping quarters were in a box in the back corner, designed to be sheltered from the wind, with a bed of clean straw, elevated six inches off the ground. I took *Lisa* into the kennel and stayed with her for a while. Monty returned with her dinner which she gratefully gobbled down. She then curled up on the straw and was happy to go to sleep.

Back in the room sorting out our equipment, I was suggesting to Ian that we might be better off moving into the spare kennel. It had better facilities. *"Never mind,"* said Ian, *"We will have our dinner and go for a few pints." "Sounds good to me!"* I said, and we went downstairs where we joined Stan and Frank who were busy looking at a stuffed otter in the sitting room. It was a peculiar looking specimen. Whoever had stuffed it hadn't quite got it right. It was standing up on its back legs as though it was stretching to see as far as possible. The mouth was slightly open and it looked as though it had a smile on its face. Monty marched in and announced, *"Dinner is ready. Follow me!"* We followed him into a small dining room where there were two tables with four chairs around each table. Only one table was set for dinner and we sat down. Monty stood guard by a cupboard door and clapped his hands twice. A young boy of about twelve came into the room carrying a tray with two bowls of soup on it. The boy had a frightened look on his face as he placed the two bowls on to the table and sped off to return with another two. Monty instructed us to begin. The soup bowls were extremely small and there was about half an inch of clear tasteless soup in the bottom of them. In the middle of the table was a plate with a large pile of sliced bread and Stan had four slices with his soup. Stan had a good appetite, often eating twice as much as most people. All the time Monty stood to attention watching us eat. When Stan had finished drying his bowl with the forth slice of bread, Monty clapped his hands again. The young boy came in and quickly cleared the bowls away. Monty asked, *"What do you think of the soup boys?"* Ian replied with great sincerity that he thought it was very filling. I had to quickly find my handkerchief and pretend to blow my nose to try and hide the fact that I was laughing. The boy returned with our main course. It was served on very small plates. The size you would give to a child. Consisting of two small potatoes, a teaspoon full of cabbage, two slices of carrot and two tablespoons of some brown stuff which I think was some kind of stew. While this cuisine was being served by the extremely nervous boy, Monty had been into the cupboard he was guarding and had produced a rifle. I thought I had better eat this or the bastard is likely to shoot us. It didn't taste too bad. In fact, there was very little taste to it. Stan was ploughing through the heap of bread while eating the meal. Eating was a serious time for Stan. He never looked up from his plate. He just kept on firing it in with both hands. When we had finished and Stan had wiped the pattern off the bottom of the plate, Monty, who had thankfully put the gun away, asked would anyone like any more. Stan immediately responded with, *"Me please!"* Monty clapped his hands and the boy, who must have been standing just outside, came in. Monty shouted. *"Fetch the rest of the stew boy!"* The boy hurried off and returned with a saucepan which contained about half a cup full of stew. Monty took the pan off the boy and walked over to Stan. There was one slice of bread left on the table and Monty instructed Stan. *"Put the bread on your plate and I will put the stew on top of it."* Stan said he would prefer to dip the bread into the stew, so would he please just tip it onto the plate. *"I will not!"* shouted Monty, *"Now put the bread on your plate or you will do without the stew."* The thought of losing the stew was a disaster to Stan and he quickly followed orders and placed the bread on the plate. Monty tipped out the remains of the stew and Stan got stuck in. When he had eaten the bread with the stew on it, there was still some gravy on his plate. Stan asked Monty if he could have some more bread to dip up the gravy. Monty replied, *"No, you have had plenty!"* and clapped his hands again. You could see the sorrow in Stan's eyes as his plate was removed, still bearing the remains of the gravy. After the boy had cleared the plates away he returned with some small dishes that had custard in them. As the boy walked around the table there was a great bellow from Monty. *"Be careful boy, when you're cornering with the custard!"* I couldn't control myself any longer and burst out laughing. The boy looked at me and produced a little nervous smile. Monty just glared at me. After a few minutes I managed to compose myself and ate my lumpy custard. I don't know how I managed to find these places, but I had done it again.

"Be careful boy when cornering with the custard!"

When dinner was over I checked that *Lisa* was all right and took her for a walk. After tucking her in for the night, I went to the pub with the boys. Ian soon got into form and entertained us and the locals for the next couple of hours. When we told the locals where we were staying, one of them wanted to bet us a fiver that we wouldn't last the week. He said we would either leave of our own accord or Monty would throw us out. He said that very few wildfowlers lasted the week in Colditz.

We returned to the guest house in good spirits. It was as quiet as a mortuary. Monty had gone to bed leaving a note on the table with our orders to be quiet when we leave in the morning. We were all pretty tired from our journey and went to bed.

During the previous week I had been studying Ordnance Survey Maps of the area where we intended to shoot. I have incurred major problems in the past, trying to obtain permission to cross farmers fields, to gain access to the foreshore. Farmers have unfortunately been pushed into a situation where they automatically refuse permission for access, due to the antics of the minority. Fences have been broken by people climbing over them, rather than walking to the field gate. When gates have been used, only too often they have been left open, resulting in sheep and cattle escaping onto the roads.

I found a track, marked on the map as a public right of way, which ran from the road and between fields, all the way down to the foreshore. It was about half a mile long. This is where we will be heading for in the morning.

When the alarm went off at six, I climbed out of bed and turned it off, feeling as though I could have slept for another five hours. I went across the hall to Stan and Frank's room. Stan was dressed and wiping the barrels of a beautiful eight bore. Frank was still asleep so I decided to waken him. It took two or three minutes of vigorous shaking before Frank lifted one eye lid. I told him it was time he was up. He just closed his eye and went to sleep again. I asked Stan to get Frank up and went back to my room to get myself ready.

Three quarters of an hour later Ian and I were downstairs, ready to go, when Stan came down and told us that Frank was still asleep. I took a glass of water from the kitchen and went up to Frank's room where I found him sleeping. When I poured half of the cold water on his face, he sat up and shouted *"What's going on?"* I told him he was making us all late and if he wasn't ready in ten minutes, we would leave him behind. He jumped out of bed muttering something about that we should have woke him earlier.

We all went in the Cortina and it took us longer than anticipated to find the public right of way. When we got out of the car, the first signs of dawn were showing. Knowing Stan's record of meticulousness, I asked him to make a big effort and get ready quickly. We were only half way to the foreshore, puffing and panting from running, when we heard shots being fired and the first skein of geese came over us. I couldn't believe my eyes when Frank started to take his gun out of its sleeve while fumbling for cartridges. I told him to put the gun back in the sleeve until we reached the foreshore, which he reluctantly did. The sight of these geese made us run faster and we eventually reached the mud. There was little cover and light was breaking fast. Spreading out, we knelt in the mud behind small tufts of grass. *Lisa* tucked in behind me. There were several skeins of geese flying along the Solway. Constantly calling, as though they were waiting for an answer from other geese, telling them where a safe exit was so they could come inland for their breakfast. It was a cold morning with little wind.

The geese eventually left the sanctuary of the Solway but not until they had reached a height of about four gunshots. However, that didn't deter some wildfowlers to our left from emptying their barrels at them.

The first skein of geese that came off would probably have been in range, had we been earlier and in position. I felt angry that Frank had caused the situation. However, my anger was put to one side as I enjoyed the views of the Solway Firth. The flight was over so I sat on a tuft of grass and soaked up the scenery. It was magnificent, with the hills in the distance and the wading birds working away at the water's edge. I decided then that I wouldn't say anything to Frank. We had a week ahead of us and I didn't want any ill feeling.

When we were walking back to the car, Frank suggested that it could have been better if we had been out earlier. I could have buried an axe into his head if I had been lucky enough to have one at hand. Instead, I just bit my lip. I was feeling disappointed but the good things were, we now knew where the track was and we had seen quite a lot of geese. If we get it right tomorrow, we may be successful.

On the way back to Monty's place we could see the geese feeding in the fields. It would be difficult to give an accurate estimate of how many we saw grazing, but I would guess at over two thousand. When we arrived Monty was in the hall, standing to attention. He eyed us up and down to make sure we were suitably dressed and retorted. *"Where's your dog?"* I told him she was in the car. *"She would be better in the kennel, now bring her round the back."* I was getting fed up with taking Monty's orders so I told him that *Lisa* enjoys being in the car so I will leave her there. He glared at me for a minute and then told us breakfast will be ready in fifteen minutes. I was pleased to hear it being ready for a good feed.

After going upstairs to wash and change, we were sat waiting at the dining room table which was set with a huge pile of bread in the centre. Stan wanted to make a start on it, but there was no butter on the table and he wasn't quite hungry enough to eat the dry bread. The young waiter from the previous night must have been at school because Monty served the breakfast himself. He brought in a tray which contained the four small plates that we had used before. On the plates was the breakfast. You may think I am exaggerating but I can assure you that this is fact. The breakfast consisted of one small bantam egg, one slice of bacon, which was probably cut down the middle and one tiny particle of a sausage, the size of a finger end. Monty must have taken a chipolata and twisted it. Then, cutting it up to make three of these sausages he was serving. It was ridiculous! I have given bigger breakfasts to my children before they were old enough to attend school. The Vicar looked at the plate and started to grin. I had to get my handkerchief out again and leave the room for a couple of minutes to compose myself. I returned to the table to find Monty had gone to the kitchen for a pot of tea. Stan was wading through the bread moaning that there was no butter. *"Why don't you ask Monty for some butter?"* enquired Ian sarcastically. Stan replied, *"I am frightened he might take the bread away."* Monty brought the tea in and put it on the table. When Ian came out with the next remark, I lost control completely. He turned to Monty and said, *"Could you let us have a doggy bag in case we can't eat it all?"* Monty must have thought he had given us too much to eat because he lifted the plate with the bread on it and vanished into the kitchen. I thought Stan was going to burst into tears. Monty didn't return to the dining room again. We drank our tea and went out to have a look around Dumfries and visit the local gun shop.

Dumfries is an old Scottish town, steeped in history, being situated on the River Nith where a wiser man than me had previously ventured, called Robert Burns. The people here were friendly and we had a good laugh, along with some interesting conversation in the local gun shop. The proprietor of the gun shop informed us of several places we could shoot, including some good duck flighting on Loch Ken. Having a memory like a sieve, I took some notes of the places he had told us about and thanked him for his help. As a thank you, I bought a hundred cartridges I didn't really need. Stan was talking about eight bores and the proprietor produced six boxes of eight bore cartridges. Eight bore cartridges were very difficult to come by and Stan was delighted when the man sold them to him.

I sometimes wonder why Stan comes with us on these shooting trips, as he certainly won't threaten the bird populations. In fact, I have only seen him hit one thing in all the times we have been out shooting together. I had negotiated with a land owner to extend our shoot at Leverstock Green. The extra land consisted of six fields. The first time we shot the fields Stan was with us. I noticed the land owner was standing at the edge of the road watching us. We lined out along the first field which ran parallel with the road and started to walk it in a straight line. Stan was on the end of the line, maybe sixty yards in from the road and had been given strict instruction not to shoot towards the road. When we were about halfway across the field, a pigeon flew along the line of guns heading towards the road. Everybody had a look at it and everyone except Stan realised it was a racing pigeon. Up went Stan's gun and he shot it as clean as a whistle. I half expected a call from the land owner to tell me not to come again. Maybe the land owner was as ignorant as Stan about breeds of pigeon because I never heard from him.

Lunch time came and we went into a restaurant (which I shall call the Ritz) for a meal and a couple of pints. The food was first class and plenty of it. I suggested that we went back to the place we were that morning on the Solway for evening flight. If we got there early enough we could organise some cover for the next morning. The boys agreed so we arrived there at three-thirty. There was virtually no cover out on the mud. The best cover was along a narrow strip of rough ground which separated the fields from the mud. We built some hides with drift wood and dead grass then waited for the flight to start. The place was alive with curlew flying in from the land and onto the mud to roost. Some of the birds were coming off the fields just a few feet above our heads. It was getting dark and not a sign of a goose. When it was almost black, we heard the geese coming. The noise from them was increasing in volume as they came closer. Although it was too dark to see them, I knew there were a lot of geese because they kept flying over us for at least ten minutes, and from the sound I would say, they were probably no more than fifty yards up and landing out on the mud somewhere not too far in front of us. As the skeins landed, the calls altered as much as to say, we have made it safely to roost. We waited until the flight was over and made our way back to the car. *Lisa* had a wash in a burn and I dried her with some towels. That was the first day over and not a shot fired.

Arriving back at Monty's place, I received instructions to put the dog in the kennels. Monty came out with a large dish of food for her which she gratefully accepted. What a strange man Monty was. The dog was fed the best of food and we were given a small portion of rubbish. We struggled through dinner that was served again by the frightened boy. Another small serving of the unnamed soup, half a cup of some sludge that was called curry and the lumpy custard had been enhanced with a dollop of jam on it.

We retired to the sitting room to allow five minutes for digestion. Stan told us he was going to find a fish and chip shop to finish off his meal and Frank went with him. Me and Ian were looking at the otter and trying to work out why it had a grin on its face. Ian said, *"It was because the otter could see the expressions on the guest's faces in the dining room when Monty served up his culinary delights."* Monty came in to the room and enquired where the other two were. Ian told him they had gone for a walk to help to digest their big meal. Monty said, *"That Stan fellow does tend to eat too much."* Monty asked us if we would like some more tea and we accepted his offer. He sat with us drinking the tea and seemed to relax a bit. He remarked on what a nice looking spaniel *Lisa* was. I told him she was a brilliant dog but a bit on the small side. He told me that most of the spaniels in South West Scotland were small and I have found over the years he was absolutely right. He asked us if we liked the otter. I told him I thought it was very good but unusually mounted. I am pleased I didn't criticise it, as he went on to tell us he had mounted it himself. He told us he had been doing taxidermy for years and offered to show us some of the things he had mounted. He unlocked a door leading off the sitting room and went through it, returning with a barnacle goose. He sat it on the table so we could view it. It was mounted in a way as though it was feeding. He then went back into the room and came back with a drake mallard and a cock wigeon sitting them on the table. He then returned with a cock pheasant and placed that down alongside the others. I must admit the birds looked realistic but the odd thing was that they were all mounted with their heads bowed down towards the ground. Maybe he mounted them so they could worship him. As I was plucking up enough courage to ask him, Ian came straight out with it. *"Why are they all mounted with their heads down?"* He told us to come into the room and he would show us. We walked into the room which was a small workshop. Along one wall was a unit with rows of shelves built into it. There must have been fifty stuffed birds on the shelves, all with their heads bowed down. Monty said, *"You can see the problem I have. If I mount them with their heads up they won't fit between the shelves."* Ian looked at me and I had to make a quick retreat to the toilet where I laughed for a good five minutes. Anybody outside the toilet door would have thought I was completely mad.

We went to the watering hole and after a while Stan and Frank joined us. Stan couldn't find a fish shop open so he had eaten a meal in the Ritz and looked contented as he read his Bible. I suggested to Frank that he might want an early night as he had so much trouble waking up. He said, *"You only have to wake me. There is no need to try and drowned me."*

I decided not to reply but I thought if you don't get up in the morning you can stay there. I told the boys about the stuffed birds and when we returned to Monty's place I tried the door to the workshop so I could show them, but it was locked. We said goodnight to the otter which seemed to have a bigger grin than ever and we went to bed.

Next morning, up at six and across to Stan's room to waken the dead. Stan was up and dressed, passionately wiping the eight bore barrels. After shaking Frank, he opened his eyes. I told him it was time to get up. He closed his eyes again. I said, *"See you at breakfast Frank when we get back"* and went back to my room. We were ready to go out of the door at a quarter to seven when Frank came down the stairs. *"Have I got time for a cup of tea?"* he said. *"Only if you want to walk!"* I said, and went to the kennel for *Lisa*. We were at the right of way in plenty of time and Stan took his time to get ready, without being harassed.

Walking down the track with a stiff breeze at our backs, we could hear the geese at their roost, chatting away to each other. God knows how they manage to sleep, as they are never quiet. We set up in the makeshift hides we had put together the day before, about fifty yards apart. Unfortunately, the only materials available for constructing a hide was dead grass and a lot of it had blown off the branches which made up the main frame of the hide. Even so, there was still enough in front of us to break up our shape and as long as we kept dead still we should be all right.

Sitting there stroking *Lisa*, waiting in anticipation, was a wonderful moment. I started to think of my children. They would be getting ready to go to school. It was Jacky's birthday today and I was missing again. My friends would be sitting in a traffic jam on the motorway trying to get to work. People will be rushing about catching trains and buses, pushing each other out of the way. A lot of people think I am mad sitting out here in the mud in all weathers, but I know where I would rather be.

With the first glimmer of light, some geese lifted to form a skein. You would think they would have learnt to be quiet by now and try to sneak inland. They made so much noise lifting you would have heard them a mile away. Although I still couldn't see them, I knew they were not very far away. I was straining my eyes and *Lisa* was wagging her tail in excitement. Suddenly, there they were, coming straight at us, about thirty yards high and forty yards to my left. I clicked my fingers at *Lisa* and she tucked in close to me and stopped wagging her tail. They started to swing towards me and my heart started thumping. Just when I thought my luck was in, they swung to the left and flew over Stan. For once Stan had remembered to put the cartridges in and the mighty eight bore blazed away with both barrels. Not a bloody feather came down and the geese flew on, shouting with some annoyance at Stan. Five minutes later another skein followed the same route and they were also saluted with the eight bore. Another skein came off a hundred yards further down and four shots from some other wildfowlers brought down three geese. Before the flight was over, four more skeins took the safe route over Stan. They were all saluted with two barrels, suffering no casualties. The geese had all gone and *Lisa* looked at Stan in total disgust.

Walking back, Stan was delighted. He had never fired so many shots out of the eight bore and he couldn't get over it. The fact that he hadn't hit anything didn't seem to bother him at all. If I had fired twelve shots at thirty yard geese over the top of me, I would be extremely disappointed if I had failed to hit one. Frank was saying very little and it was pretty obvious that he wasn't enjoying himself very much. I think he expected to shoot geese on every flight. I have always had the philosophy about goose flighting. Don't expect anything and you won't be disappointed.

While driving back to Monty's palace for our mini breakfast, Ian was passing remarks to Stan like, *"Your shooting wasn't too bad. I think you frightened one of them!"* Stan said he thought one of them was going to come down. Ian replied, *"It will probably come down when it is hungry."* When breakfast was over, we went to the sitting room to discuss the day's tactics. Stan said, *"The first thing he was going to do was go to the Ritz for another breakfast."* Monty came in and sat with us and said. *"You boys have been very good and I am pleased with you. I am taking you rough shooting tomorrow, after you have had your breakfast.* What a man! He never asked us if we wanted to go. He just told us we were going and none of us had the courage to argue.

Joining Stan for a proper breakfast, I suggested that instead of going for the geese that night, we could go to Loch Ken for evening flight and try our luck at the duck. Stan and Frank had come to shoot their first goose and said they would prefer to go back to the Solway. I could understand their point, although, I think Stan could sit under the geese for a month and never hit one. Ian said he fancied the ducks so we were to split up for evening flight.

While walking around Dumfries it started to rain quite heavy. Ian suggested that we should find a pub with a roof that didn't leak and have a couple of beers. While enjoying the crack, we got into conversation with some other wildfowlers who were taking refuge from the weather. They told us they had spent the previous week shooting on Wigtown Bay, where they had seen thousands of pinkfeet. I remembered looking at Wigtown Bay on the map. It was about fifty miles West of Dumfries. I decided I would go and see it for myself before we went home. We had been instructed by Monty that we were rough shooting tomorrow, so I asked Ian if he would go with me on Thursday. Stan had arranged to collect the car door on Thursday from somewhere in Ayrshire and Frank was going with him.

Me and Ian set off for Loch Ken at two in the afternoon. When we arrived we found the cottage where the shooting permits were issued. A most helpful and friendly man gave us our permits and spent a great deal of time explaining to us the best places for shooting duck. He also told us there was a good chance of a goose coming into the loch to roost.

We had plenty of time so we drove to the village of New Galloway which sits at the head of the loch. Finding a tea room, we had a quick snack and then back to the loch to find a suitable position for evening flight. The rain had eased off but it was definitely feeling colder with a strong wind. Ideal for duck flighting I thought. We found a peninsular with some bushes on it and from the amount of empty cartridges laying around, it looked like a favourite spot. I put my hand in the water to check the temperature. It could only have been one degree above freezing. When *Lisa* saw me put my hand in, she decided to have a little paddle. The cold water never seems to bother her, yet, when I give her a nice warm bath she stands there shaking with fear. At first I thought she was frightened of the slippery bath surface under her feet. I placed a mat on the bottom of the bath but it made no difference. Whenever I mentioned the bath she would lay under the table trying to make herself as inconspicuous as possible.

The peninsular wasn't very wide so we were about thirty yards apart. I sat and watched some tufted duck swimming around and diving. It is incredible how long they can stay under the water. Among the other residents were some grebes and a small family of swans.

It was getting dark and the cold was starting to bite. *Lisa's* tail wagged and seconds later a bunch of teal dropped straight into the loch twenty yards in front of me, with such speed, that I never had a chance to mount the gun. I clapped my hands and they sprung vertically into the sky. Ian took one out as they swung over him and it dropped behind. Moments later five mallard flew past me with the wind behind them. They were going like bullets. I swung through the front bird and dropped the one behind it stone dead with a big splash. *Lisa* wanted to go but I made her wait. I heard the whistle of wigeon as they flew past us and managed to shoot a bird at the back of the pack. This was tremendous shooting! The ducks were screaming in at what seemed like ninety miles an hour. In ten minutes I had fired sixteen cartridges and was pleased to have shot six ducks. *Lisa* collected the ducks and delivered them with her usual high standard. We had shot ten ducks between us and it was one of the most exciting flights I had been on.

On the way back to Monty's house of pleasure we were chatting. I suggested that we should give the evening meal a miss at Monty's one night and have a good steak in the Ritz instead. Ian thought it was a good idea and we decided to ask Stan and Frank to join us. I was thinking about Monty's dinners and wondering if we would be offered a different soup tonight. If he had made just a small pan of soup at the beginning of the week, it would easily last the six meals with the quantities he was serving. I can put up with the tasteless soup if only he would give us a decent pudding. I am beginning to tire of the lumpy custard.

Stan and Frank were in their bedroom when we arrived at Monty's haven. After we had hung up the ducks in an outbuilding, we went up to see them. They told us that the geese came back to their roost on the Solway the same as the previous night. Plenty of them but too dark to see them. We told them about the ducks at Loch Ken and you could see the disappointment on Frank's face because he had missed out on a good flight. It would be nice if he could shoot his first goose this week. At least he is learning they don't come easy. I told them about our idea of having an evening meal at the Ritz one night. They both agreed it was a good idea. We decided to go on the Friday night, which would be our last evening meal in Scotland.

Sat at the dining room table in anticipation, we were waiting to see what delights were in store for us tonight. Monty came in and took up his position on guard and with the usual signal the boy came in with the soup. It was the same as before except someone had put a spoonful of garden peas in it. Ian said convincingly. *"This looks good!"* Monty replied, *"We like to vary the menu!"* We ate the soup with the centre of the peas still frozen and prepared ourselves for the next course. The boy came in with the small plates containing a thin slice of haggis, a dessert spoon full of swede and the same amount of mashed potato, which turned out to be lumpy. I could read the expression on Stan's face. He looked at the heap of dry bread on the table and there was nothing on his plate that he could dip it in. The lumpy custard followed, this time decorated with chocolate strands, which I have always called, chocolate mouse muck.

An hour later we were in the watering hole getting stuck in to a large plate of salmon sandwiches and a couple of pints. I was starting to feel the pace and very tired. Whenever I returned home from a shooting trip, I was totally shattered. It usually took me a couple of weeks to recover. An early night was on the menu and I slept like a log.

Next morning when we were walking down the track to the foreshore, the wind was howling. It had changed direction and was blowing across us. Settling into our hides, which had lost all of the dry grass, we waited. The geese were out there chattering away as before. This morning, for reasons I didn't understand, the geese didn't lift until it was almost light. I could actually see them on the mud three hundred yards in front of us. Surely this is going to be the day when we score! They periodically lifted to form small skeins and headed straight towards us, gaining height as they flew. Although they were trying to fly over us, the strong cross wind was blowing them sideways. Skein after skein crossed a hundred yards to my left. I would have moved position but there were already several wildfowlers there, and they were having a field day. In twenty minutes they had killed a dozen geese, whilst we never fired a shot. When we were walking back to the car, Frank suggested, that we should get out early tomorrow and take up position where the geese had been shot. I told him he could if he wanted to, but it is more than likely that the wind would change and the geese would come off somewhere else. Frank still didn't realise that you have to be very fortunate to be in the right place to shoot geese on the foreshore. It's entirely different to decoying geese into fields, where you can encourage the geese into range.

We arrived back at the car which Ian had parked on the grass verge. Ian reversed the car into the track to turn round when a tractor came along the road. Ian waited for it to pass before pulling out. The tractor stopped right in front of the car and the driver climbed down from the cab and walked over to the car. After winding down the window Ian said with a smile, *"Good morning!"* The man looked in the car at us and stated, *"You shouldn't be on this ground. It belongs to me! you ken."* I was prepared for such an incident. Producing the O. S. Map, I pointed out to him that it clearly indicates that this track to the foreshore is a public right of way. With this the man became angry and shouted, *"I am not interested in your bloody English maps, you ken. I am the Laird and this land belongs to me!"* This brought a reaction from Ian which I found hilarious. *"A Laird, a real Laird! Please, let me shake your hand. I have never met a real Laird before!"* Ian extended his arm out of the window and the man looked at it confused by Ian's response. He took Ian's hand and tentatively shook it, as though he had just got hold of a lump of dog dirt, and went on to say. *"If you boys give me five pounds each, I will let you go, otherwise, I will go and fetch the police, you ken,"* Ian laughed and replied, *"You must be joking! If you was a proper Laird, you wouldn't need the money."* He then followed it up with, *"You ken."* The man's face turned crimson with fury, not sure what to do. He looked at the car and then at his tractor. We were hardly going to sit there and wait while he went in his tractor to fetch the police. After a while he said, *"Where are you boys staying?"* Stan said, *"You will always find us in the Ritz at meal times."* The man shouted, *"You will be hearing from me! you ken,"* as he walked to his tractor, Ian shouted, *"I will look forward to it. It's not everyday you meet a Laird."* As the tractor drove off we roared with laughter. No geese, but the crack was good.

Back at Monty's five star accommodation, we had breakfast. Today on the plate, along with the bantam egg and morsel of sausage, was half of a tinned tomato. Unfortunately, the bacon had been taken off the menu. Monty said, *"When you have finished your breakfast we will be off. It will take half an hour to drive to the farm where we will be rough shooting."* Well it certainly won't take us long to finish our breakfast, I thought. I had seen more food on a cream cracker! I could see Stan was concerned because he was going to miss his proper breakfast in the Ritz.

Following Monty's car, we eventually turned off the road, down a track and pulled up outside a beautiful period farmhouse. After a ten minute walk we came to some ground that had a series of small woods on it. Monty told us, *"We will begin here."* He put me on one side, Ian on the other side and took Frank and Stan inside the wood to take it through. You would think that with me being the only one with a dog, I would have been inside the wood, working my dog. Maybe he didn't want the pheasants flushed and shot. He probably takes his paying guests here every week. As we set off walking I noticed a cock pheasant, which ran out of the bottom of the wood and into the next wood. When we started on the next wood, it did the same thing again. The pheasant certainly had worked it out, because when we drove the last piece of woodland, the pheasant flew out of the bottom and back to where we had started, staying about a hundred yards out to my left. That was the only pheasant I saw all day. After all that excitement we started walking up moorland. A big hare got up in front of me and I received a bollocking from Monty for not having a shot at it.

After a couple of hours, Monty said, *"We will cut across these fields and go back to the farmhouse for lunch."* That's more like it I thought. It was a lovely building, and I could imagine the farmer's wife serving up a first class lunch. When we arrived at the farmhouse, instead of taking us in, Monty took us round the back and into a dark coal shed. There were some old fish boxes laying around. Monty told us to sit on the boxes and he would fetch the packed lunch from the car. He came back with a flask and a sandwich box. The box was half the size I use for myself, when I am working. I was thinking, he must be going to perform the miracle of the loaves and fishes if our lunch is in that box. Unfortunately, he had never been taught about miracles in the army. All we had was one small sandwich each, which contained a very thin slice of haggis that must have been left over from dinner the night before.

Bellies still empty, off we went again on another route march. We were walking in a straight line over boggy ground, with me at one end and Monty at the other end. I knew Monty was shouting something to me but I couldn't make out what it was. Ian was the next in line to me so I asked him what Monty was shouting. *"Get further out."* Ian said. I walked further out and now Monty was screaming and waving his arms about. I asked Ian again what Monty was saying. Ian said, *"I was only kidding. He really wants you to come in,"* and he burst out laughing. I came in closer and Monty calmed down.

During the course of the afternoons walk, we put up half a dozen snipe. Two got up in front of me and I let them go. When I was served snipe on toast in Islay, I vowed I would never shoot one. To me they are so small, with such little meat on them, it doesn't warrant the killing. At the end of the day I received another bollocking for not shooting at the snipe. By now, it was like water off a duck's back. I had enjoyed the walk over new ground but the sad thing was, we had missed evening flight. If I had been offered a choice between the day's rough shooting or an evening flight on Loch Ken, Monty's little route march would have come second best.

Waiting at the dining room table we were so hungry. I think we would have eaten anything. Our starter was served. Thank Goodness the tasteless soup had eventually run out. We were given half a slice of toast with a teaspoonful of pâté. Ian said, *"Things are looking up boys. We are on solids!"* Monty glared at him and Ian took no notice. Stan even managed to stretch the pâté to a thin smearing on a slice of bread. Ian said, *"Go steady Stan, you won't have any room left for your main course."* I had to cover up with my handkerchief again. The ingredients of the main course were, a small dollop of lumpy mashed potato, two slices of carrot and a couple of spoonfuls of some white liquid that we were told was fish stew. The nearest to fish I got out of my portion was a bone and a piece of skin. Stan took full advantage of the liquid and managed three slices of bread with it, before Monty removed the bread from the table. Tonight the lumpy custard had some little silver balls sprinkled on it.

We filled up later with sandwiches in the watering hole and were entertained by a couple of men playing Scottish music. One had an accordion and the other a fiddle. The more we drank the better the music sounded. The other wildfowlers we had met earlier in the week were in there. We had a good laugh exchanging experiences. Frank and Stan went back to their beds just before ten but me and Ian stayed until they finally closed. We were in real good spirits by now, where every little thing seemed to be amusing. Arriving back, we went into the sitting room and passed stupid remarks about the otter. I went to the cupboard in the passage and took Frank's football scarf and hat. Carefully, I dressed the otter. It looked a treat! I decided it could do with the jersey and a pair of shorts. Going up to Frank's room I stole his football shirt from a chair. Taking a pair of jockey shorts from my bag, I went back downstairs. Being careful not to damage the otter, I put the shirt on it and wrapped the shorts around it, fastening them at the back with a safety pin. The Otter looked great. I wish I had taken a photograph. The only thing missing were the football boots. Ian pushed an unlighted cigarette in the otter's mouth and we fell about laughing. We decided to leave it dressed up until the morning so we could show Stan and Frank.

When we got up in the morning the otter was gone and so was Frank's kit. What we didn't know then, but found out later was, Monty had a part time job, working between four and eight in the morning at a local bakers. The reason for the large quantities of bread on the table was now apparent. He must have seen the otter when he got up for work and removed it.

When we went outside we were surprised by two inches of snow everywhere. The wind was howling and the snow was swirling around. *Lisa* came out of her box to meet me. I thought she might be cold but when I felt her she was warmer than me. The traffic on the road was crawling and by the time we reached the right of way, we were late. I told the boys we are going to have to run or we will miss the flight. Ian said he couldn't face running as he was feeling a bit rough from the night before. He got back in the car and told us to go without him as he was going to have a sleep. The wind was blowing the snow horizontally into our backs as we ran down the track. I heard a skein of geese come off before we reached the mud and light had broken by the time we reached the hides. I had just put the cartridges in when I heard the geese out in front. *Lisa* tucked in tight and I kept dead still. The geese were flying straight into a blizzard so I decided to call them. I remembered the previous day when they were on the same flight line and then veered off to my left. I kept calling and they were calling back. In a way I felt sorry for them. They were heading straight into an ambush. When they were twenty five yards out I swung onto a bird and killed it stone dead. Just as I swung through the second bird, the mighty eight bore went off from seventy yards away. The bird I had swung through jinked as I pulled the trigger. Although I hit the bird, it wasn't dead. It plunged sideways out of the skein and hit the mud a hundred yards to my left. *Lisa* wanted to go but I told her to stay. There were a lot of geese coming off the Solway, and I didn't want to spoil the shooting for other wildfowlers by sending my dog out in the middle of the flight. *Lisa* was disgusted when we saw a black Labrador run out and pick up the goose I had shot.

Even though I didn't get another shot, it was a bad morning for the geese. The blizzard had kept them low and they paid the price. I saw about ten geese shot to my left and I could hear shooting right along the shore line. Three skeins came off over Frank and Stan during the flight. Six cartridges were fired into the air but nothing came down.

The flight was over and the snow had eased off. I walked along the mud to where my goose had dropped. When I reached to where the Labrador had come out from, I stopped and looked. Behind some dunes were four wildfowlers with a heap of dead geese. I walked over to them. The man with the Labrador was a big fat ugly looking specimen. I said good morning to them but they just sat there grinning to each other. These wildfowlers definitely belonged to the inferior fifty percent. I spoke again. *"Thank you for sending your dog out for my goose earlier."* The fat man puffed at his cigarette and replied with a grin, *"I don't know what you're effing well talking about pal. We haven't seen your goose!"* I told him I saw his dog go out and retrieve it. He had another puff and said, *"I shot the goose the dog brought back. Your effing goose is still out there!"* I knew he was lying but to pacify him, I sent *Lisa* out. She returned quickly and gave me the look that meant there was nothing there. I looked at them for a minute. They were smirking away as much as to say, we have got your goose and you can't do a thing about it. I said, *"I hope you don't waste the goose."* I could hear the fat man laughing as I was walking away. It's at times like that when you can understand how people are murdered. I felt like turning round and blasting that big load of useless blubber into the mud and out of existence but I would like to class myself among the better fifty percent of wildfowlers and kept on walking.

When we returned to the car, Ian was surprised to see that we only had one goose. By the amount of shots he had heard he thought we would have had half a dozen. He said that the geese were still in range as they were flying over the road.

Back at Monty's house of fun, I hung the goose up in the out building, alongside the ducks and went to my room. I could hear Frank downstairs, pleading with Monty to return his football kit.

Monty reluctantly returned it, but not without giving Frank a lecture on how to behave in other people's houses.

We went down and sat at the dining room table ready for breakfast. Monty burst into the room and shouted, *"Who shot the goose?"* I reluctantly admitted that it was me, expecting a bollocking. He shouted again, *"You will have two eggs this morning!"* and walked out. Well, I did get two eggs that morning but the tight fisted sod never gave me the morsel of sausage that the others got. Eating our proper breakfast later in the Ritz, we laughed at Monty's generosity. This happened twenty-five years ago and I still have to smile when I think about it.

That afternoon Stan and Frank went to Ayrshire to pick up the car part that Stan was so excited about, and me and Ian went to have a look at Wigtown Bay, in Wigtownshire. As we drove westwards along the A75, I noticed how the traffic slowed down and the place seemed so peaceful. Getting closer, there was the water of the Solway leading into Wigtown Bay on our left, while on the right there were mountains climbing out of the Galloway Forest, which seemed to be endless. This was an area of peace, tranquillity and great beauty. As we drove around the bay there were cottages dotted here and there along the coast line, with geese flighting over them. How I envied the occupants of those cottages living in such beautiful surroundings. I decided then that next winter I would have a week shooting on Wigtown Bay. It would be nice if Tony and The Greg could join me and Ian. We drove into a little market town called Newton Stewart and had a cup of tea in a café. Nobody seemed to rush about. The pace of life here was much more sensible than that of the South of England. I noticed that the young people mixed freely with the old, having interesting conversations in the café. The young people where I lived had no time for the elderly. They never stopped to think that one day, if they are lucky enough, they would be an old person themselves.

We decided to have the evening flight on Wigtown Bay and went out onto the foreshore at Wigtown, from an area called the Martyrs Stake. Not being familiar with the area, we were reluctant to venture too far out onto the mud. After crossing a couple of deep creeks we decided to take up our positions and wait. A few minutes later, three wildfowlers walked past us and went a long way out in front. Not knowing the tides, we decided to stay where we were. As darkness drew in, some wigeon screamed over my head from behind. A pure reaction shot sent one of them down into the mud.

Lisa brought it to me and it looked like a mud ball. The geese were coming into roost, passing over us two gunshots high. We sat and watched them. What a wonderful sight watching pinkfeet flying in. They are constantly changing places in the formation and jostling for position while calling to each other. Hearing shots out in front, I wondered if we should have followed the other wildfowlers we saw earlier. Another pack of wigeon and another mud ball delivered to hand by *Lisa*. Not a shot at a goose but an enjoyable flight.

    I could hear water slushing about and realised the creek we were standing in was filling up. We made a hasty retreat back to the car, crossing the deep creeks with a foot of water in them. Back at the car we were changed and ready to go when the three wildfowlers we had seen earlier, came off the mud. They were soaked and looked frightened. The water in the last creek they had crossed came up to their waists, filling their waders with muddy water. We lent them some towels and gave them some hot coffee from a flask which had been filled in the café at Newton Stewart. They were grateful for our help and told us that the water was coming in quicker than they could come off the mud. I was pleased we were cautious and never followed these guys out. During conversation they told us that they had gone out to the water's edge, where one of them had shot a goose. Unfortunately, the goose had dropped in the water and they didn't have a dog. The tide started to come in and they waited because they thought the tide would wash the goose in to them. They realised just in time that the tide was filling up the creeks behind them, cutting off their escape route. As it happened, they were lucky and they only lost the goose. If they had stayed out there any longer who knows what the results would have been. Before we said cheerio, they gave me the name of the person where they were staying for the week. His name was Sid and he lived in a traditional four bedroom granite house, which was also the village shop. Over the years I have stayed at Sid's house on many occasions, having some wonderful shooting trips in this area. Although Sid doesn't live in Scotland anymore, I still communicate with him to this day.

    Arriving back at Monty's paradise, we were just in time for dinner. Another batch of the clear tasteless soup had been created. The stew that caused so much trouble for Stan the first night, was back on the menu. I think the lumpy custard must have been made in a forty-five gallon drum, because it was served up yet again, this time decorated with half a cherry. Never mind I thought, tomorrow night we are going to the Ritz for a big steak. The problem is, who is going to tell Monty?

The next morning the weather conditions had changed again. The wind had dropped and the sky was clear, leaving a cold frosty morning. We were in good time on the foreshore and took up our positions. The geese moved very early, with the first skeins coming over well in range. I didn't fire at them, leaving a chance for Ian and Frank and they both shot a goose. Stan could have sat there until this time next year and he still wouldn't have hit one. The guns to the left of me opened up and a goose glided down onto the mud in front of me with a badly injured wing and leg. It started to try and make its way back to the water but was in great difficulty flapping about. I sent *Lisa* out and she returned with the goose, which was nearly as big as her. I quickly dispatched it, putting it out of its misery. When the flight was over, my friend the fat man, was wandering about out in front of me with his dog. I shouted across holding up the goose, *"Is this what you are looking for?"* He stood there looking at me, not sure what to do. He didn't have his gang with him this morning and he wasn't quite so brave. He slowly came over to me and I held out the goose for him. He took it with a puzzled look on his face, muttering a muffled thanks, as though he found it difficult to say. I replied, *"It's my pleasure! Wildfowlers must try to help each other if they can."* He grunted and wandered off looking totally confused. I hope he learnt something from my gesture but I doubt very much if it would influence an ignorant lout like him.

At breakfast, Ian and Frank were treated to two eggs, but they suffered the same fate as I had with the sausage. I asked Ian if he would tell Monty that we would not be in for evening meal tonight. *"Certainly not,"* he replied, *"I have upset him enough."* We had a major problem here. Four grown men and we were all too frightened of Monty to tell him.

For lunch we went to the watering hole, still trying to determine who was going to risk life and limb and tell Monty. We decided, because nobody would volunteer and nobody would accept a bribe, the fairest way was to draw straws. We all agreed to this and I took four matches and broke a quarter of an inch off one of them. I told them, *"The one who ends up with the short match tells Monty."* Turning with my back facing the boys, I placed the four matches between my finger and thumb leaving the ends sticking out evenly. I turned to face them again and I have never seen such worried-looking faces in my life. I held my hand out containing the matches and asked, *"Who would like to go first?"* They looked at

I have never seen such worried-looking faces.

each other, then at me, then at each other again. Eventually Stan took hold of a match. He then let go again and studied them. He took hold of another one, closed his eyes and pulled it out. He opened his eyes and realised he had a full match. The look of joy on his face was indescribable. I can only relate it to how Barrabas must have felt when Pilate reprieved him from crucifixion, instead of Jesus Christ. The joy on Stan's face was the opposite to the concern on the faces of Frank and Ian. Following Stan's success, Frank and Ian decided to get it over with and went to grab the matches together. I pulled the matches away and told them to go one at a time. Putting my hand out again Ian was the first in and pulled out a match. A big roar of laughter from Ian confirmed that he had been lucky. I was beginning to think that the luck of the Raw was just around the corner when Frank pulled out the short match. He looked at it with disbelief, unable to speak. His mouth was opening and shutting as though he was trying to talk but nothing was coming out. He eventually took a mouthful of beer and composed himself.

Taking a deep breath he announced, *"I know I drew the short match but I am not going to tell Monty. I wanted to draw the match that Ian drew and Vince wouldn't let me."* I have never seen a man look so relieved as Frank did when we all started laughing. I suggested that there was only one thing we could do. We would eat at Monty's and then go for our steak. We all agreed and booked a table at the Ritz for eight o'clock that night.

Evening flight passed with no success and later we waded through the Belsen rations that our host kindly ordered us to eat. It was later that night when the biggest surprise of the week occurred. We were enjoying a good steak in the Ritz when, in walked Monty dressed in kilt and sporran with a lady on his arm who looked frightened to death. They were escorted by a waiter to a table at the other side of the dining room. The waiter pulled out a chair for the lady who sat down after receiving the orders to do so from Monty. We felt guilty eating our second meal with the commander watching us and finished as quickly as possible. When the waiter brought the bill, I asked him if Monty was a good customer. He replied, *"He never misses a Friday night meal, but even better for us, he must recommend our food to his guests because they all eat in here when they stay in his guest house."* We laughed all the way back. If only the waiter knew why the Ritz was so popular with Monty's guests.

Loading up the vehicles the next morning I couldn't believe the heap of rust Stan had travelled miles to obtain. It was a car door with a big rusty hole in the middle. He was delighted with it. He said he could fill the hole and paint it. The real bonus was that the hinges were not rotten and the ones on his car were. After loading, we went into the dining room for our final breakfast and Monty presented us with our bill for the week. He had charged us plenty for every conceivable thing, including packed lunch in the coal shed on our rough shooting day. He even charged us for the cup of tea he offered us before showing off his collection of bowing birds.

I would like to think that I am not a vandal but I couldn't resist slightly altering the sign in the garden of Monty's palace. In black letters on a white background was the sign saying **BED & BREAKFAST.** I made a small insertion with a black marker pen to alter the sign to **BED & NO BREAKFAST** and we headed back home towards the M6.

Two days later I was sat in a traffic jam on the M1, trying to get to my work, thinking about the Solway foreshore and who will be there this morning instead of me and the fat man.

CHAPTER 9

Meeting Sid

You will probably think by now that I am clean mad. If there is still any doubt in your mind consider this. Me and Tony are heading up the M6 to Scotland for two duck flights. A round trip of about seven hundred miles on the off chance that there may be some ducks on Loch Ken.

It was a Friday in mid September and Tony had four days off work. I should have been at work but after giving the matter some serious thought, for five seconds, I decided against it. Our plan was to arrive at Loch Ken early afternoon, collect our permits and shoot evening flight. We would find bed and breakfast and shoot morning flight, then, as Tony would put it, we will bimble off back home.

We were travelling in Tony's jeep with *Lisa* and Grobally, in the back. Well they are now. I had a strenuous fight with Grobally to determine which one of us was going to sit in the front. Every ten minutes Grobally would push between us and look out of the windscreen to check if he recognised any of the countryside. The dogs soon get to know a certain route if there is some shooting at the end of it.

I had recently bought a brand new Volkswagen pickup truck and was still running it in. It had a bench seat in the front to take three bums. Under the floor of the flat bed back was a massive lockable compartment, which the salesman suggested, was ideal for putting my tools in. I liked the look of this compartment. It was ideal for putting my gun and shooting equipment in. I was very proud of this vehicle, having run old bangers since I had taken on the mortgage, and spent more time pushing than driving them. I decided to have sign writing on the doors. Being a member of the Federation of Master Builders, I decided to have their emblem painted under my name. The emblem was a circle with writing around the inner side of the circumference. The sign writer arrived and started to work. He wrote my name across the door, which looked great, but when it came to the emblem it was a different story. Instead of a nice circle, he had painted it egg shaped. I politely pointed out to him that it is supposed to be round and was angered by his reply. *"It's just a bloody old builder's wagon!"* I couldn't believe my ears. Obtaining this vehicle was a great achievement to me and I wanted the job doing right. I lost my cool and shouted at him, *"It is not a bloody old builder's wagon, and if you don't put that emblem right, this not so bloody old builder will take that brush off you and push it somewhere where you won't like it."* He looked at me and realised I meant it. He wiped the egg off, muttering to himself, and then painted the perfect circle. The truck had only done eight hundred miles, so I didn't fancy a long drive to Scotland in it. When it was run in, it would be my shooting wagon, occasionally used for work.

As we drove up the M6 we were talking about pigeon shooting. I had been pigeon shooting with Tony many times during the closed season, on his ground at Letchworth and surrounding areas. One of the first times was in February. The weather at that time was atrocious with snow and blizzards. A farmer had made a telephone call to Tony requiring his services. He had a massive field of Brussels sprouts and the pigeons were devastating them. Tony invited me to join him and I of course accepted. While I was shovelling the snow off the drive to get my car out of the garage, my wife was grumbling. Apparently, she couldn't understand why the weather was too bad for me to take her to the shops, which were a mile away, yet I was about to venture out on a twenty-five mile journey to sit out in the snow. I must admit she had a good point so, instead of putting up a defence I decided to stay silent. After I had refused to answer her questions for the third time she went back in the house and slammed the door. That was that problem over! Now all I had to do was get to Letchworth.

The side roads were extremely tricky but once I reached the main roads they were not too bad. It was a twenty mile an hour crawl all the way, arriving at ten-thirty as agreed.

A pleasant half hour followed in the kitchen, drinking tea with Tony and Pat. It was really cosy in their kitchen and it always seemed so homely. Pat enjoyed listening to us rabbitting on about shooting and guns. I don't think she understood why we always wanted to venture out in the foulest of weather any more than my wife did, but if we enjoyed it, that was good enough for Pat.

The farm we were heading for was about six miles from Tony's house and it wasn't long before we were on our way in his jeep. When we arrived we pulled up at the side of the road and looked at the field of sprouts. The pigeons were there in their hundreds. It must have been the only food available to them because all the other fields were under six inches of snow. Tony drove the jeep down a track through the field and parked it in a small wood. As we drove down, all the pigeons lifted off and flew to a wood about half a mile away. We decided to set up a hide in the sprouts with a camouflage net.

Loaded up with guns, hide poles, nets and cartridges we set off through the sprouts to find a suitable position away from the road. The snow started again, blowing horizontally with the wind. After only walking thirty yards I noticed a large flock of pigeons heading towards the sprouts. We crouched down and they came straight in. Either they didn't see us or they were too hungry to care. They landed on the sprout tops. The closest would be about twenty yards from us and they went back to about sixty yards, with just about every sprout top with a pigeon on it. Tony told me to fire into them and put them up. I quickly removed the gun from the slip and loaded it firing the first barrel at one of the sitting pigeons. As they all lifted the sky was black with them. It was impossible to try and pick one out so I fired the second barrel into the bunch. The results of this may take some believing, but Tony will vouch for me. I shot one pigeon with the first barrel and twelve with the second.

We stayed there for two hours until the pigeons decided to call it a day and find some sprouts elsewhere. We had shot fifty-six pigeons and the sad thing was, not one of them was fit for eating. Their breast bones were prominent having very little meat on them. We took them to the game dealer and he gave us a quarter of the going price. He said they were only fit for dog food. It was a shame they were causing so much damage creating the situation where we had to shoot them.

The cold spell lasted for another two weeks. During that period, Tony picked up lots of pigeons while out walking his dogs. They had become so weak with the cold and lack of good food they were falling out of their roosting trees, dead. I was beginning to get hungry myself, so eventually I conceded and took my wife shopping.

Another time at the pigeons that sticks in my mind was with a man called Sam, who knew Tony and me. Sam had suffered from the results of a most unfortunate accident, while on holiday. He fell and broke a bone in his back, which had left him severely handicapped. It was a terrible shame because Sam really enjoyed his shooting. He still came to the clay shooting and shot 'down the line,' sitting in his wheelchair. He could cope with that, but found it extremely difficult to swing the gun sideways.

The pigeons were feeding on peas that were just germinating into young tender seedlings. Me and Tony had shot at them for the two previous days, taking one-hundred and twenty birds without making any impact on them. It would seem that the pigeons were prepared to risk their lives, to have a feed on the peas.

Tony invited Sam to come with us. Sam was reluctant to accept because of his handicap. Tony insisted and told Sam we would look after him.

I took Sam to Tony's in my car with his wheelchair folded up in the boot. With the aid of crutches, he joined us in Tony's kitchen for the usual pot of tea and chat with Pat. I could see from the expression on Sam's face that he was pleased to be with us, and couldn't wait to get at the pigeons. His pot of tea was gone in a minute. He probably thought, if he drank it quickly we would leave the kitchen and go to the pigeon shooting. I could have told him that tactic wouldn't work. I tried it the first time I was in Tony's kitchen, itching to get at the partridges. Sam achieved the same results as I did when Pat filled his pot up again with more tea. Tony will not be rushed. He likes to take his time and do things in a relaxed manner. As far as Tony is concerned, the tea drinking with Pat, before the shooting, is just as important as the shooting.

Half an hour later we were on our way. Sam in the front of Tony's Jeep and me in the back with the wheelchair and Grobally, who was intent on pushing me out. The jeep turned up a farm track, which was running alongside the pea field, with a hedge between the track and the field. We had built a hide in the hedge the day before, which was suitable for Sam. After helping him into the hide and into his wheelchair, we adjusted the branches so he could shoot out across the field. We even provided a suitably shaped stick which he could use as a gun rest. After placing twenty dead pigeons out as decoys, we walked across the other side of the huge field and left him to it.

What we saw from the opposite side of the field we found extremely amusing. We were watching the pigeons going into the decoys in front of Sam, who must have decided that it would be too difficult to swing the gun through to shoot them as they were flying, so he would shoot them as they landed. From where we were, it looked as though the pigeons were landing in a mine field. A pigeon would drop in between the decoys. As it touched the ground there was a big bang and a puff of feathers flew up in the air, as though the bird had exploded on impact with the ground. One after the other they landed on this minefield. Me and Tony were counting down as the pigeon came in to land. *"Five, four, three, two, one, zero."* Trying to get the zero to coincide with the bang.

After an hour we went back and tidied up the battlefield. There were pigeons lying dead all over the place. Sam had nearly run out of cartridges so we gave him another box and went back to the other side of the field. We had some good sport shooting the pigeon that were escaping over the hedge which we were standing in.

A couple of hours later we collected the pigeons off the field, loaded Sam into the jeep and headed back to Tony's house, stopping at the game dealers on the way to sell sixty eight pigeons. They were in prime condition for eating and most of them were going to be exported, to end up on a table in some French restaurant, fetching about fifty times the price that we had been paid.

When we walked into Tony's kitchen we were greeted by the most wonderful smell of pigeons roasting in the oven. Pat cooked us a dinner that could only be compared with the quality of her home made bread. We took our time over the meal, listening to Sam telling the story of his accident and the number of unsuccessful operations he had undergone to try and improve the situation. Pat provided a bottle of home made wine and Sam seemed to like it. I have indulged in Pat's wine in the past, only to suffer a headache for the next three days, so when I was offered some I politely refused.

We were chatting away and Sam was halfway through another bottle of wine when he decided he wanted to buy Tony a bottle of whisky as a thank you present. He asked me if I would go and buy one from an Off Licence shop for him. I told him I would but the Off Licence closed at eight and it is now eight-thirty. Tony told me where I would find a pub with a little room on the side where they sold bottles to take away. I found the pub with the little room on the side and bought a bottle of whisky. I think the landlord must have been saving up to go to the Bahamas by what he charged me for the bottle. At that time, a bottle of whisky was under six pounds. I arrived back at Tony's house with the whisky and Sam asked me how much he owed me. I told him I had better share the cost with him because it was an expensive whisky. Sam asked me what kind it was. I told him, I have called it *'Hastings'* because the robbing bastard landlord charged me *ten sixty-six.*

An hour later I took Sam home. If the police had seen him I think he would have been charged with 'drunk in charge of crutches.' Me and Tony have had many laughs reminiscing about the mine field and the bottle of 'Hastings.'

We were now on the A75 heading towards Dumfries, passing Powfoot where we have had some good goose shooting in the past on the Solway coast. On through Dumfries we turned off the A75 heading for Loch Ken. The road runs parallel with the loch and we stopped half way along it to give the dogs a run. It was a typical September evening with the air chilling after a reasonably warm day. The dogs were excited and *Lisa* kept looking at me as though she wanted to get on with the shooting. Grobally had found the remains of a bag someone had left behind after a picnic and was busy tearing it to pieces to find out if any of the contents were fit for eating.

We collected our permits from the cottage. The man in the cottage remembered me from the previous January when I had an evening flight. If this flight is anything like that one was I will be delighted.

Going into New Galloway we called at a café for a meal, which was served by a stout woman who was really cheerful. While serving the meal she never stopped talking and laughing. As she put the tea pot on the table after the meal, Tony took a large flask out of his bag and said, *"Could you put four cups of coffee in the flask please?"* The lady said, *"Certainly, I will do it now"* and walked off towards the kitchen. When she was half way there Tony shouted after her. *"Excuse me!"* the lady turned around to see what he wanted. He said, *"No sugar in two of them please!"* The lady replied *"Certainly"* and set off again. She had only taken a few steps when she stopped in her tracks and swung back round to face us with the most puzzled look on her face. To her delight we burst out laughing and she then realised we were teasing her.

I took Tony straight to the peninsular on Loch Ken where I had been successful before, where we made some hides and settled in to wait. As it became darker I could see the glow from the end of Tony's cigarette. *Lisa's* tail wagged and seconds later I heard wing beats behind me. A dozen mallard flew past me and started to circle over the loch. They were a good forty yards high when they came over me for the second time. I thought they were still a bit too high and decided to let them go round again. As they passed over Tony, two cracks from his gun had two birds falling down dead in the air and splashing into the water. Grobally went in for a retrieve so I let *Lisa* fetch the other. It can be a problem shooting with someone like Tony who is a good shot. What is a bit too high for me, is just right for him. When it became a bit darker we were on an even keel because it was impossible to see the birds at forty yards. Another bunch of mallard on my left and I took one out as they flew low over the loch, closely followed by another bunch on which I scored a right and a left. Tony was on my right and the ducks were all coming in from behind and to my left. As I fired, they were swinging away to the left and Tony wasn't getting any shooting. I let the next bunch through and he scored twice again. The dogs were loving it. We let them retrieve as the ducks were shot. Another bird each and it was dark and that was the flight over. A long journey to get there, but well worth it.

Back at the jeep we enjoyed some coffee from the flask while feeding the dogs. Now we had to find somewhere to spend the night. When I had an evening flight last January on Wigtown Bay, I met up with some other wildfowlers. They recommended a man called Sid for accommodation and gave me his telephone number. I found the number in my diary and phoned him from a public phone box. A man with a high pitched voice answered the phone. It was Sid. I asked him if he could accommodate us and was pleased to hear that he could. It took him about a quarter of an hour to give me the directions to his house describing every house and telegraph pole that we would pass on the way. In actual fact he called them 'tallywag' poles.

Half an hour later we arrived at Sid's house, which was also the village shop. As we pulled off the road and alongside the house, outside lights came on at the back. A tall man, who was a bit thin on top and wearing a brown overall came towards us. He had a welcoming smile on his face with his arm extended to shake hands when he was still five yards away. He said, *"Hello and welcome. I am Sid. Come in and have a warm in front of the fire."* I asked him if he had a kennel for the dogs. *"No kennel! Just bring them in with you."* We followed him into the house through the kitchen, into a hall and turned left into a small sitting room. The kitchen and hall were cold but the sitting room had a log fire, burning half way up the chimney. Sid put a rug down in front of the fire for the dogs. With no hesitation they laid on it and were asleep in minutes. Sid said, *"Sit down and tell me who you are, where you come from and how you got hold of my number."* While I was telling him, he reached into the cupboard next to his chair and produced a full bottle of whisky. He interrupted me to ask if we liked whisky and I told him we did. He took the top off the bottle and threw it into the fire and said, *"We won't be needing that again."* He then produced three glasses and a jug full of water from the kitchen. Half filling the glasses with whisky he said, *"Help yourselves to the water."*

Sid was a most interesting man and certainly knew about wildfowling. Apparently, he had been a guide in the area for years. Although he didn't take people out anymore, he still had many contacts and I learnt over the years he was highly respected by everybody he knew. He told us he still occasionally went out for morning flight after the geese with his friends. They rented the shooting rights on a farm that ran down to the foreshore which had three good flight ponds. When he wasn't working in the shop or shooting, he was a part time gamekeeper for another shoot.

We talked until the early hours about shooting and shared experiences. Eventually, the bottle was empty and we retired to bed, but not before booking in with Sid for a week, the following January.

We arrived at the peninsular on Loch Ken early the next morning and were disappointed to find two other wildfowlers in the hides we had built. It was dark and therefore difficult to find another suitable place. After walking down the bank of the loch for twenty minutes day began to break. We stood in some bushes about fifty yards apart. It wasn't long before the guns opened up from the peninsular. Every time the guns went off I thought the birds might swing back over us but I didn't even see them. During the course of that flight, over twenty shots were fired from the peninsular. I didn't fire a shot and Tony fired one, killing a teal. That was it, time to head back home. I would have liked to have stayed for another flight but the clay pigeon club had organised a fund raising event for that evening, which I had to attend.

CHAPTER 10

A week at Wigtown Bay

The arrangements had been made for me, Tony, Ian and the Greg to stay at Sid's place. Hopefully to shoot geese on Wigtown Bay and maybe a few other places that Sid had said he would arrange for us. There was always a chance that it was the whisky talking when Sid told me and Tony about the different places he was allowed to shoot on and all the people he knew. We would soon find out because the time to pack the motor had arrived.

Unfortunately, a couple of days before, The Greg had to pull out because of a bereavement. After a meeting we decided that just the three of us would go, instead of trying to recruit another person at such short notice. My pickup truck was to be the transport. I telephoned Sid and told him the situation with The Greg, offering to pay something to compensate for any financial loss this would cause him. He was very understanding and wouldn't accept anything.

At that time there was some crisis going on in the Middle East creating a petrol shortage. All the garages in our area were rationing petrol, with massive queues waiting to get to the pumps. It was ridiculous! After a half hour wait in the slow moving queue, you reached the pump, only to be told you were allowed one gallon. The vehicle had damned near used a gallon of petrol while waiting in the queue. I was concerned that we wouldn't be able to buy fuel in Scotland when we arrived so I spent days filling cans to take with us on the back of the truck. None of the garages would allow the filling of cans. You put the rationed petrol in the vehicle's tank and went straight to another garage to join another queue. I siphoned the petrol out of the vehicle into cans. I heard of a garage in a village near Dunstable that was allowing three gallons per vehicle. I made several trips to that garage until I had enough petrol in the vehicle and cans to take us to Scotland and back again, with enough spare to do a fair bit of running around while we were there.

The lockable compartment under the flat bed back of the truck was quite large, but not really large enough to take the equipment of three wildfowlers, heading off for a week, so some things had to be left behind. The amount of clothing Ian's wife had packed for him would have filled the compartment without anything else. As usual, eighty percent of it was left behind. Waders in plastic bags went on the back along with my hide and some nets. Three men could sit comfortably in the cab but there wasn't much room left for dogs. Poor Grobally had to stay behind but we managed to squeeze *Lisa* in with her being half the size of Grobally.

I bought *Lisa* as a seven week old puppy from a man who regularly wrote articles on dogs in a magazine. He was advertising three Springer spaniels that were ten months old with basic training, ready for more serious training. A friend of mine who earned far more money than me, had recently got the shooting bug and had joined a syndicate. He soon realised he needed a dog and asked me if I would go with him to see these dogs that were advertised. It was about seventy miles from Dunstable and we went in my friend's car.

When we arrived at the breeder's house he took us into the back garden which had a row of kennels with runs. There were several dogs in the kennels leaping up the wire runs when they saw us coming. The three spaniels that were for sale were in a run together. They were fine looking bitches all from the same litter. Well built and fairly long in the leg, having good eyes and ears, with well proportioned liver and white markings on a clean shiny coat. He put them on leads and we walked from his house and across the road onto some heath land. He then let them off one at a time and demonstrated their skills. For ten months old they were impressive. My friend knew little about working dogs and asked me to pick the best one out. I watched them for an hour before I decided on one, although I considered the asking price was far too much being far more than I could have afforded. My friend wasn't bothered about the price and wrote a cheque out for the chosen bitch.

Before we left, the breeder was trying to talk me into having one of the other two. I told him I would very much like another spaniel as the one I had was eleven that year but I couldn't afford the sort of money he was talking about. He took me into a shed to show me another spaniel. She had given birth to seven liver and white puppies the day before. I asked him how much the puppies would be and he told me fifteen pounds. He took me into the house showing me the pedigree. It is impossible to select a puppy at a day old and with him being such an authority on dogs, I respected his judgement. I asked him if he would save me a good bitch out of the litter and paid him the fifteen pounds. He said he would ring me when she was ready to leave her mother.

Seven weeks later I received a call saying she was ready. My friend, who had bought the ten month old spaniel, said he wanted to go and see the breeder about some query he had about the pedigree so he would bring my puppy back with him.

What a little thing she was! My first impression was I had been given the runt of the litter. That didn't really bother me that much because I have seen the runt of the litter make the best working dog out of the litter. What bothered me was, she was so small and so miserable. The next day I took her to the vet for a check-up. The vet was horrified with her condition. She was infested with lice which were embedded into her private parts. He informed me that the only effective way to get rid of the lice was to dip her, as they do with sheep. He went on to say that to dip her at her age would kill her. He said he would try and control the infestation with a powder until she was six months old and then he would dip her.

Over the next five weeks I took her to the vets twice a week. It was obvious that she wasn't developing as she should. She wasn't interested in food or playing. I told the vet that in my opinion she was getting weaker each week, and I didn't think she would live to be six months old. He examined her and said I could well be right, but to dip her now would be a great risk.

I laid awake that night trying to make a decision. The poor little pup looked at me as though she was saying, *"Please help me!"* I decided to take a chance and have her dipped. I had to sign a paper at the vets saying it was my decision.

After the dipping she was extremely poorly. I spent over a week nursing her all night like a baby. She wouldn't eat and just laid in her basket shaking. She also lost control of her bladder. I put nappies on her and wrapped her in warm towels, sitting up for hours nursing her in my arms. I tempted her to eat with high protein foods and she gradually took more and more. I knew after two weeks she was going to make it. Unfortunately, she missed out on those important months when the bone structure develops. During the fight to save her, we formed a bond that would never be broken. I honestly believe that she had given up but stuck in there to please me. She was a great little dog. I often wonder what size she would have grown to under normal circumstances.

The vet wrote a letter to the breeder telling him what he thought of him. The breeder replied stating that it was inevitable that some pups would have lice. The vet was so angered by this lack of concern from the breeder he reported the matter to the R. S. P. C. A. I don't know what the outcome was, but I hope it led to improvements in the conditions that his breeding stock were reared in. I couldn't understand why the three ten month old bitches had been in such good condition and my pup was so bad. I found out later from my friend that the ten month old bitches were reared by someone else. He was just selling them for him.

As we were heading up the M6 the atmosphere in the truck was great. Ian suggested that we should stop at one of the service stations and sell some petrol. He said I probably had more on the back of the truck than they would have in their pumps.

I had a radio cassette fitted in the cab. We were playing all the latest music. A group called *'Boney M'* had recently brought out a great record called, *'By the rivers of Babylon'* I had bought the cassette and played it constantly with the volume up high.

It took us seven hours to reach Sid's house but it seemed to fly by. What I did notice was, once we had crossed the border into Scotland there was no petrol shortage. It was business as usual in the garages, you could have what you wanted. The luck of the Raw! I must have swallowed a gallon, siphoning petrol out of my truck into cans every night for the last week.

Sid was pleased to see us and made us welcome. There was a woman called Elsie who helped him in the shop and she cooked the meals when he had guests. They were soon given the nickname of El-Sid. The food was good and plenty of it. While we were eating dinner Sid was stood talking to us. He had the most strange way of standing. He seemed to push his pelvis forward and lean his shoulders back. While he was talking, rattling out one story after another, he had his hands in front of him, covering up his private parts, like the football players do when forming a wall. I don't know if he had received a boot in the painful place in the past, but every time he stood to talk, both hands protected the three piece suite.

When we had finished dinner I gave Sid a bottle of whisky. I told him it was to replace the one we drank when we were there in September. He took the bottle and said in his high pitched voice. *"It doesn't mature with age once it has been bottled. We had better drink it!"* We followed him into the sitting room and finished the bottle in front of the log fire.

He told us that a lot of geese had arrived in the area in the last week. Apparently the geese initially head for the East coast in Perthshire. As the weather gets harder they cross to the West coast where it is usually warmer, benefiting from the warmth of the gulf stream. He suggested that we shoot the foreshore in the morning. In the afternoon he would take us to one of the farms where he has permission to shoot geese, to see if there were signs to indicate that geese were feeding there. If they were feeding there we could go the following morning. Things were getting better and the whisky was making me feel contented. Sid said he would have to find some nettles for his arthritis. I asked him if he boiled them. He said, *"No, I pick them and beat myself with them."* Most people grow flower beds. Sid grows nettle beds, pulls them up by the handful and knocks seven shades out of himself. If he enjoys it, fair enough, but to me it seems a pretty drastic way to relieve arthritic pains.

It soon became obvious that Sid had his own vocabulary. I remembered last September when he was giving me directions, he was talking about 'tallywag poles'. Tonight he was talking about different people who have stayed with him. He said. *"One week I had 'Three Gun Cyril' staying and the next week I had a couple of 'gerrycatrics' who flew in on an 'airyplane'."*

I was in bed by twelve. Lying awake for some time wondering about morning flight. Every so often a lorry drove past, probably heading for Ireland via the ferry terminal at Stranraer. Each time the house shook a bit. I felt relaxed and soon fell asleep. It's funny how whisky relaxes me.

Next morning we were up and excited. Sid had made a phone call the night before, to let a farmer know that we would be crossing his fields in the morning on our way to the foreshore, He had drawn us a map on a piece of the paper that he uses for wrapping the bread that he sold in the shop, describing how we could find the farm. He initially started to tell us the way but after twenty minutes of passing 'tallywag poles' and 'tellingbone' boxes, he lost me, so I asked him to write it down.

We were soon in the truck and heading for a farm at a place called South Balfern in an area known as The Machars. The weather in Sid's garden seemed mild but when we got out of the vehicle at South Balfern the wind was quite strong. Obviously with being situated on the foreshore it was more exposed to the elements. The lights were on in the farmhouse and in the barn adjacent to it. The farmers work many hours in a week. Probably twice as many as most people in the city.

We found the gate that Sid had marked on the map and set off across a field coming to a gate at the other side. This gate was also marked with great detail, even to the extent of detailing the fact that the bolt was broken and it would be tied with string. I tied the gate and we crossed another field. Climbing over a stile at the bottom of the field and walking alongside a small wood, we were on the foreshore.

Lots of gullies, getting deeper and deeper as we walked towards the water's edge. The tide was out and according to the tide table it would start making its way back in about ten-thirty. We kept walking until the mud became very soft where we split up and found suitable gullies about fifty yards apart.

I could hear geese in the distance chatting away to each other at their roost. I thought, they could be late leaving their roost this morning because the tide won't push them off early. The wind was quite strong but blowing across us. Not the ideal conditions. I had carried two pieces of wood with me and wedged them across the gully, making a seat and somewhere to stand, without sinking up to my knees in the mud. It was still dark and I sat watching the headlights of the lorries driving along the A75 on the other side of the bay.

At the first sign of light, gulls were coming off in their hundreds just a few yards over our heads. The curlews and oyster catchers were busy working the shore line. It never fails to amaze me that, nearly every living thing in the sea is some other creatures breakfast.

It was nearly light when the first skein of geese took to the air with the usual noise and excitement. It was so light I could actually see the geese roosting on a mud bank in the middle of the bay. There must have been a thousand of them. The skein of about fifty pinkfeet came straight towards us. Although I have been in this position many times I still get a tremendous thrill with the anticipation of success. I went through the check list in my head. *"Push the safety catch off when ready, keep still and don't move until ready to fire, swing the gun, don't poke it."* If I don't talk to myself I always forget something. The geese were coming over the shore line about thirty yards up. They were still a hundred and fifty yards from me but coming in nicely. When they were a hundred yards away they suddenly climbed up and swung round, heading parallel with the shore with the wind behind them. Something frightened them but I didn't know what. I looked along to where Tony and Ian were and they were tucked in tight. It was when I looked behind me that I saw the problem. A farmer was working his collie dog, rounding up the sheep in the last field we had crossed.

Five minutes later a goose lifted out of a gully about twenty yards to my right. It was flying with difficulty and never lifted more than ten yards. Landing at the water's edge it started foraging with the oyster catchers. I came to the conclusion that the goose must be injured. Maybe from some out of range shooting. I had read that once a goose suffers an injury it is chased away by the other geese. I suppose it is all about survival. The geese don't want a passenger in the skein.

More geese were starting to lift, forming large skeins. Although two skeins did come over me after I called them, they were stretching range. The majority of the skeins flew along the bay for about two miles with the wind behind them, before they turned right and flew inland. Skein after skein followed the same flight line until the flight was over.

First morning flight and not a shot fired. I did make a point however, of noticing where the geese turned inland. It was where the shore line jutted out into the bay by some tall trees. I intended to speak to Sid about it over breakfast.

We returned to the vehicle and I took a bottle of whisky to the farmer. I found him in the barn with his arm up the back end of a ewe. After he had pulled a lamb out and wiped it on the ground and then onto the ewe's face, she took over the job of washing it. He washed his arms in a bucket of disinfected water and was pleased to receive the bottle. He asked me if we had shot any geese. I told him they went the other way. He said, *"They must of seen you boy. They always fly over the farm in a morning, you ken."* I didn't have the heart to tell him it was him they had seen. As I was walking away he said. *"Come any time you like, you ken. But you will have to make sure they don't see you, you ken."* I smiled and thanked him and we went back to Sid's for breakfast.

Sid's helper cooked an excellent breakfast while Sid worked in the shop. When it was ready, she took over in the shop and Sid came into the dining room to talk to us while we were eating. I told him what had happened on morning flight and where the majority of the geese had gone inland. He smiled and went into his leaning back posture. With his hands protecting his wife's wedding present, he announced. *"That's Orchardton farm where they came off. That's where we rent the shooting rights. We will have a flight there one morning. I am going to take you there tonight for the duck."* He went on to tell us that he would take us to Castle Douglas in the afternoon to check if the geese were feeding there but first he had to have a session with the nettles. He kept some in his greenhouse away from the frost. He told me that the Romans used nettles to relieve pain when they built Hadrian's Wall. I'm a great believer of 'When in Rome do as the Romans do,' but this is Scotland!

We all piled into Sid's Morris traveller and set off for Castle Douglas. Sid was telling us that the geese in the Castle Douglas area are nearly all greylags, while on Wigtown Bay they are nearly all pinkfeet. There was the odd skein of barnacle geese about, but they were, and still are protected.

We turned off the main road, drove two miles along a side road and turned up a steep farm track for about half a mile, before pulling into a farm yard. The farmer and dairy man came out to see who had pulled in. When they saw Sid they came over and shook his hand, wishing him a happy New Year. Sid told them what we intended doing. The farmer said, *"Go ahead, the geese are a damned nuisance!"*

Walking across four fields away from the farm we came to the brow of a hill. Looking down, there was a strip of land two fields wide and three fields long. The fields the other side of this strip climbed up again to form a valley. We walked down into the valley. The fields were littered with fresh goose droppings. The geese must have been there that morning. Tomorrow, we will be waiting.

Back to Sid's for a cup of tea and to get ready for an evening flight at the duck. I love chasing the geese but to me the ducks are far better, particularly the wigeon. Late in the afternoon a friend of Sid's arrived. His name was Alan Dimmock. He was in the same small syndicate as Sid and was going with us for evening flight.

By the time we set off in the vehicles, the day was trying to close. We drove past South Balfern and on a straight road for another two miles to Orchardton Farm. The wind was still strong and fleecy white clouds were rushing across the sky. Alan told us they had three ponds. They had shot the one behind the wood the previous week, so that left one in front of the wood, which was good for mallard and teal, and another by a derelict cottage that was good for wigeon. Sid took Tony and Ian to the pond in front of the wood and I went with Alan for the wigeon. I was delighted with the arrangements. I would exchange ten mallard flights for a good wigeon flight.

After a quarter of a mile walk we were at the pond. It was an old mill pond but looked more like a flash. There were several varieties of plants growing out of it including Flote grass and Tassel pond weed. As Alan was showing me where to stand, the guns on the other pond opened up. Alan said, *"That will be the mallard. They always come first. The wigeon should be here in about five minutes."* I stood in some gorse bushes about twenty yards back from the flash. *Lisa* gave a little whine of excitement and lay with her head looking through a hole in the bush. The moon was coming up behind a mountain called Cairnsmore, on the other side of the bay. As it lifted above Cairnsmore it lit up the flash. Conditions were perfect for wigeon flighting and they arrived within minutes. When I am shooting with someone for the first time, I am reluctant to shoot first so when the first pack of wigeon flew over the flash, I left them. Alan took one as they screamed out. He shouted, *"Don't wait for me, just shoot them when you see them!"* Seconds later another pack of wigeon from the opposite side. Alan fired at them and they swung out straight over me at ninety miles an hour. I took one out in front and swung the gun so fast over my head to fire the second barrel, I lost my footing. I didn't make contact with the wigeon but I made contact with the gorse bush which deposited a dozen spikes into to my backside. It was me who gave out the whine this time, but it wasn't with excitement. More wigeon and we opened up together. Three wigeon hit the water from four barrels. I thought the flight was over when another pack screamed over my head from behind. I took a right and a left which I was pleased with. They were a good height and if it hadn't been for the moon against a fleecy sky, we would never have seen them. They came down in the field at the other side of the flash, so I sent *Lisa*. She was back in no time, pushing one into my hand and then away again. Alan said we had shot enough so I put the gun away and picked up the empty cartridge cases. *Lisa* still hadn't returned from the other side so I walked round to help her find the duck. As I walked round I saw her sitting staring at something. A closer look with the torch revealed the wigeon I had shot was splattered firmly in the middle of one of the biggest cow pats I have ever seen. *Lisa* had no intentions of picking it up. She had decided to sit and guard it until someone, who was stupid enough to pick it up, arrived. I picked it up and took it to the flash to wash it. While I was there the wigeon were still screaming in.

While we were walking back, the shooting was still going on at the other pond. Alan said, *"That will be the teal. They always come late!"* Alan claimed a right and a left out of the three we shot together. I didn't say anything but I thought I had shot two of them. It is possible that we both fired at the same bird together.

Ten minutes later the others came across the field to join us. There were smiles all round. They had shot five mallard and four teal. Me and Alan accounted for ten wigeon, when we stopped shooting. I was pleased that we stopped when we did. In those conditions we could have carried on shooting much longer, but ten is enough.

After we had dinner we were sat around the fire listening to Sid's stories. He told us that one time he took three wildfowlers out to a farm where he had permission to shoot the geese. The farm bordered a large estate and the boundaries were split by a burn. The estate employed many gamekeepers and one of them was notorious for his ignorant and abrupt manner. This particular morning, the three wildfowlers had shot a couple of geese each and were happy. Just as they were about to leave, another skein of geese came over quite high. Sid hadn't taken a shot that morning, leaving the shooting to his guests, so he decided to have a shot at these. He made contact and the goose angled down and dropped in some rushes at the other side of the burn. Sid told the boys to go back to the car and wait for him while he went to retrieve the goose. He put his gun in the sleeve and placing it on the ground he waded across the burn. After searching he had just found his goose when a Landrover pulled up and three keepers jumped out. Mr ignorant was one of them. He grabbed Sid's arm and took his goose saying to the other two. *"Go and search those bushes at the side of the burn and find his gun."* The two keepers went to this little copse of bushes and searched them. They were soon back telling Mr ignorant that there was no gun there. That's when Sid got out of his pram. He grabbed his goose back and said, *"Of course there is no gun there, it is on the other side of the burn. I am not a bloody poacher and I have every right to come onto this land, without my gun, to retrieve my goose. Wait there and I will show you where my gun is!"* Sid waded back across the burn and when he reached his gun he held it up. *"That's my gun and I will be writing to the head keeper to complain about your attitude!"* While Sid was telling this story he became quite excited and we had to laugh. He stood up waving one arm around while the other was covering his private bits.

I was in bed by eleven, looking forward to the next morning at Castle Douglas. *Lisa* lay on a cover in the corner of the bedroom. It was like heaven to her. She could sleep with one eye closed and keep the other one looking at me.

Up like a lark and raring to go. Ian made the tea while I took *Lisa* outside. It was cold, windy and dry. The moon had gone and it was pitch black. We loaded some decoys into the truck from out of a shed and we were on our way. When we arrived at the farm it was still black. The dairy man came out of the shed and told us the geese came back in yesterday afternoon, just after we had left.

Walking across the fields we came to the valley. After setting the decoys out, we lined out behind a dry stone wall, called a 'Stane Dyke' in Scotland. Ian on my left and Tony on the right with his cigarette glowing away in the dark. A bunch of teal flew past us as day was breaking and we watched them go.

It was nearly light when the geese arrived. I heard them long before I saw them. I wondered if they were just passing in the distance but the noise was definitely sounding closer. They were about half a mile away when I saw them as they swung over a hill and headed to the valley. I started to call them and they were calling back with excitement, flying in the perfect formation. I pushed myself tight into the stone wall and kept calling. I didn't dare look up because it was now light. I knew they were close but they had to pass Ian first. I heard Ian's gun fire and lifted my head in time to see a goose falling out of a skein of about two hundred. They climbed up, swinging away over Tony who took a right and left with ease. The geese shouted at us as they flew off into the distance and soon were out of sight. Geese fly a lot faster than you realise. You only have to look at how quickly they are out of sight to see this. Anyone who has shot at geese will tell you that ninety-five percent of geese missed are missed behind.

We waited for the next skein but we had to wait a long time. Plenty of geese were moving in the distance but it was half past nine when the next skein came. A quarter of the size of the first skein but exactly the same route in. Ian scored again but this time the geese swung away from us, not offering a chance to me or Tony. We waited for another half hour but it had gone quiet. Not a goose in the sky anywhere so we collected up the decoys and headed back for breakfast. I named the place 'goose valley' and have shot there many times since.

Over breakfast I was telling Sid about the flight and I could see his eyes light up as I explained the way the geese were coming in. He said, *"If you want to go back there tomorrow I will come with you. The lady who helps me, works in the shop on a Wednesday morning."* I thought we might be pushing our luck to try the same place two mornings on the trot after frightening them today, but when I saw the enthusiasm on Sid's face, I couldn't refuse.

Sid told us, if we wanted, we could have evening flight at a flooded wood that he feeds. He had said it was good sport trying to shoot the mallard and teal as they fly over the trees although there wouldn't be a large bag. I told him the bag size didn't matter and we of course accepted his offer. A detailed map was drawn on another piece of bread wrapping.

We were at the wood in plenty of time. It was about three hundred yards long and fifty wide being flooded in places with about nine inches of water. We split up and found a flooded part each. The trees were hanging over the flooded area with gaps of two or three yards between the branches. I found a dry elevated spot to wait with *Lisa* beside me. The little dog looked confused. This was pheasant country, not duck.

I was looking at the canopy, waiting for the ducks, when two teal flew in from the side between the trees, jinking like woodcock. They landed on the water before I had a chance to move. They were swimming around looking nervous as though they sensed my presence. A moment later a shot from the other side of the wood sent them flying out just three feet off the ground. They obviously hadn't heard of a springing teal. A few moments later two mallard dropped in through the trees. They seemed to appear from nowhere and far too close to shoot. Just before it was dark two mallard flew over the wood at a good height. I could see their silhouette in the gaps through the trees. I swung through the front bird and it folded. The bird behind jinked to the right and I never saw it again.

The flight was over and *Lisa* picked a difficult teal for Tony. Ian had two shots but without success. I must admit it was fun but I would rather be at a flash after wigeon.

Another night round the fire telling stories. I thought I was bad, but Sid has got even more stories than me.

Next morning we were in for a surprise. When I took *Lisa* out, it was snowing, with a couple of inches already settled. Sid took his own vehicle because he wanted to go on to Dumfries after the shooting. Ian sat with him to keep him company. It was a slow journey but we had allowed plenty of time. The closer we got to Castle Douglas, the deeper the snow was. As we drove up the steep farm track the wheels were spinning. I think the vehicle would have made it if Sid hadn't stopped in front of me to speak to one of the farm workers who was walking up the hill.

Sid tried to get started again but the wheels just spun. Ian jumped out and he and the farm worker pushed the car up the hill. I had no chance of starting again. My vehicle was much too heavy to push. I reversed down and had another run at it. The virgin snow had now been flattened and polished by our efforts in the truck and after three attempts I abandoned the idea.

When we were leaving 'goose valley' the morning before, I had noticed a road a few fields away. I thought, that must have been the road we turned off to climb up to the farm. I found a lay-by on the road and we walked from there. I was sure I knew where we were, so instead of walking all the way round the roads to go back to the farm, I threw the bag of decoys on my back and headed across the fields. It's amazing how everything looks so different when covered in snow. We found 'goose valley' and set the decoys out on the snow. Standing behind the stone wall we waited for Sid and Ian to arrive. As the first sign of light came I was starting to worry. No sign of Sid and Ian. I walked across the valley and up the other side. When I reached the top and looked over the hill there was another valley, exactly the same as the one we were in. I stood there for a few moments and shouted for Sid. His head popped up from behind a stone wall. I realised then we were in the wrong place. I ran back down to where the decoys were and Tony helped me collect them up. Twenty minutes later we were with Sid and Ian. It still hadn't completely broken light so we put the decoys out and lined out behind the stone wall about fifty yards apart. This time with me on the end, with Sid next in line, then Ian and Tony. Surely I will be lucky this morning, it's my third flight and still no goose. I had built up a sweat running with the decoys and now I was starting to feel the cold. I was standing in five inches of snow and it was still coming down thick and fast. It had now broken light and not a goose in the sky. Yesterday we had seen thousands of geese but today they must be staying on their roost.

My feet were beginning to hurt from the cold. It's an awful feeling when your feet are so cold they start going numb and yet the pain underneath them is unbearable. You find yourself standing on one leg like a stork, and when the pain gets too bad in that foot, you change legs.

I was determined to get a goose this morning and was sure it would only be a matter of time before the geese came to have a look in the valley. The dairyman had told us they came back in on Monday afternoon. I kept looking at the watch and wondering how much longer I could stick the pain in my feet. Nine o'clock, half past nine, ten o'clock. It was about quarter past ten when I was about to give in when I saw them. A dozen greylags popped over the hill straight across from me. I expected the geese to come from the left, as they did yesterday, but there they were out in front, fifteen yards off the ground and not a sound from them. I crouched in tight and looked through a hole in the stone wall watching them coming towards me. My heart started pumping. This was it. I was going to get a goose. On they came, silently flying through the snow. Just another forty yards and you are mine. The luck of the Raw struck. The geese seemed to stop in their tracks and climb vertically. They then swung around and headed back the way they had come. They couldn't see me, so what could have frightened them? I looked to my right and couldn't believe what I saw. Sid was marching alongside the stone wall towards me. As he got closer he held out a little box he had in his hand and said those famous words that I have never forgotten. *"Do you want a sweetie before I go?"* I know what I felt like doing with his sweeties but I bit my lip and counted to ten. I asked him if he had seen the geese. He said, *"What geese? It is too late for the geese to come now. I am going to Dumfries!"* I couldn't stand the pain in my feet any longer and we went back for breakfast.

We went to the foreshore for evening flight at a place called 'The Crook of Baldoon.' The main object was wigeon flighting but we took a few number ones in case the geese came over us. Following Sid's directions, we walked across the fields to a wood, over a wooden bridge and followed the fence down towards the water's edge where there were some flashes. *Lisa* ran into a clump of rushes alongside the fence to flush a pheasant. She then gave out a loud cry followed by plenty of yelps. She had touched an electric fence. Turning her head she looked at me as though I had done something to her. At least we now know the fence is switched on. People say that electric fences don't hurt you but I wouldn't fancy resting my scrotum on one.

"Do you want a sweetie?"

Finding three flashes, we split up. The sky was packed with cloud and it became dark very quickly. The wigeon came late. I managed to shoot one in the first pack but after that I couldn't see them. I could hear them flying over and dropping into the flash. *Lisa* was enjoying it, so I sat there for another half hour just listening to them. A skein of pinkfeet came over me calling constantly. I wasn't sure how high they were and I thought I could make them out in the dark but decided not to shoot. That was the flight over. A wigeon for me and Ian. Tony never dirtied his gun. *Lisa* kept well away from the fence on our way back. She kept looking at me to make sure I never did anything to her like she thought I had before.

When we were drinking the whisky that night, Sid told me that I was on another farm that morning when I first set out the decoys. It just shows how easily a mistake can be made. I wonder if the judge would believe such a story.

Sid was very apologetic about frightening the geese. He genuinely hadn't seen them. To make up for it, he had been on the phone again to a keeper friend in Stranraer. He had arranged a morning flight for us at the geese. He told us the keeper isn't allowed to charge for taking people out but we should unofficially give him something. Out came the bread wrapping again and another detailed map was drawn. We had to go to the keeper's cottage in the morning. The snow wouldn't effect the shooting as it was near the coast and the salt air prevents the snow from settling.

 The next morning we were on our way, giving ourselves plenty of time to cope with the roads. The snow ploughs had been busy during the night and the roads were pretty clear. The atmosphere in the cab was great, with the music playing loud and we were singing along with it. We pulled off the main road and along a track turning right through an archway and pulled up outside the keeper's cottage. During the hours of darkness, in this part of Scotland, it is so quiet, a lot of the visitors can't sleep. Well, it was quiet here until we pulled up. We came upon the cottage quicker than expected from the detail on the map and we still had *'The rivers of Babylon'* blasting out of both door speakers. The noise that followed was horrendous. There must have been ten dogs in kennels which started barking as loud as they could. This chorus was added to by some geese in the garden and to make matters worse, we were half an hour early. I turned the lights and cassette player off and we sat in the cab listening to the noise from the animals. After about a quarter of an hour they settled down and it went quiet again. We had sat there nearly half an hour and not a sign of lights in the cottage. I was getting worried. If the keeper could have slept through that noise in his garden he could well sleep until dinner time.

 I asked Tony if he would knock on the door. He looked concerned but walked down the short path. The cottage was really old, looking like something out of a Frankenstein film. The door was massive, towering above Tony as he cautiously ventured towards it. He looked back towards us nervously, wondering how he had got lumbered with the task. He stood and looked at the door and then back towards us. We beckoned him to knock on the door. He held his hand near the door, for what seemed like five minutes, then tentatively tapped on it. This brought no response from within and I was not surprised. It was such a quiet tap I don't think the mice would have heard it. Tony looked back towards us as much as to say, *"Can I come back now?"* We waved our arms beckoning for him to bang on the door harder. He reluctantly turned towards the door which must have been eight feet high and four feet wide. It looked as though it could have been a draw bridge and someone had filled in the moat. Tony shrugged his shoulders and banged his fist on the door four times. Well! The bloody chorus from the animals let loose again. I don't know which was loudest, the chorus from the garden or Ian laughing in the cab. This time a light came on in the hall and a voice from the other side of the door, which sounded like a giant, roared, *"Wait a minute!"* The decibels from the voice made Tony leap back in alarm. The giant on the other side started to unfasten the door, rattling locks, chains and bolts for a good five minutes. There must have been ten locking mechanisms on it. The door slowly creaked open and Tony looked petrified. It opened to reveal a giant of about four feet nine inches high. He opened his mouth and bellowed at the dogs causing Tony to leap back again. The dogs immediately stopped barking and the geese also shut up. The miniature giant looked at Tony and roared again, *"I will be ten minutes!"* and pushed the door closed. When Tony got back in the car, we were in stitches from laughing but Tony looked quite shaken.

Ten minutes later the keeper came out with two spaniels. With the instructions bellowed out of, *"follow me!"* he got into his van and drove off up the track. I followed him along the track for about a mile and pulled up behind him. The keeper said, *"Walk across this field until you come to a stane dyke. Line out along the dyke and the geese will fly over you. When I say, stop shooting, you stop shooting."* With that, he jumped in his van and drove off. We laughed after he had gone. What a miserable little fellow we had found here.

We were soon marching across the field and found the stone wall. Ian stopped first then Tony and I carried on about seventy yards. As the light was breaking I could see we were on like a plateau. There was about twenty yards of flat ground either side of the wall and then the ground just dropped away.

It wasn't long before the geese came. I had two skeins of greylags over me in no time but they were too low, being only ten yards over my head. When the third skein came at the same height, I waved my arms at them to get them to lift. As they went up vertically, I took one out and it dropped over the edge of the plateau out of site. I sent *Lisa* for it and she soon returned struggling with a goose that was as big as her.

I could hear Tony and Ian taking a few shots. As it became lighter the geese flew higher. I shot another two and put my gun away. Three geese are plenty on one flight. As Lisa came back onto the plateau with the last goose, I saw another spaniel come up behind her and then turn away. I walked to the edge to look over and could see our giant friend picking up with his two spaniels. He was picking the geese as the boys shot them.

Twenty minutes later the giant was at the start of the stone wall shouting for us to stop. Tony and Ian jumped over the wall to go and collect the geese that they had shot, which were out of site down the slope. They didn't know that the sly little sod had already picked them. They had only walked about ten yards when the roar from our friend came again. *"When I say, 'that's it', I mean it, now come away from that dyke!"* Tony and Ian followed orders and we walked to our vehicle. The keeper was standing by his van. Tony tried to explain that they hadn't picked their geese, only to be hollered at again *"There's no bloody geese there. I am going back to the cottage!"* If it hadn't been for the fact that Sid had organised this treat for us, I would have straightened this little Hitler out. I told the boys that he had picked their geese and they could have one of mine. We went back to the cottage and the keeper was standing there. I asked him how much we owed him. He said, *"I don't charge for taking people out. I did it for Sid!"* Tony and Ian had given me ten pounds each so I offered him thirty pounds for his trouble. His face lit up as he took the money and his voice dropped to the normal decibel count when he said. *"Did you all get geese boys?"* Tony told him that he and Ian never got any because he wouldn't let them pick them. *"Never mind about that!"* he said, as he opened the back doors of his van. *"You can have some of these!"* I don't know how many geese the boys had shot but there were at least eight geese in the back of the van. He gave them two each, shut the van doors and went inside his cottage. When me and Tony reminisce we always give this story the title, *'The rivers of Babylon.'*

When we returned for breakfast Sid had another surprise for us. The young man, who owns the shoot where Sid is a part time gamekeeper, lives in England. He had rung Sid to tell him he had come up to stay at the shooting lodge for a few days and asked if Sid would come over for a rough shoot. Sid had told him we were staying there and he told him to bring us along with him. Sid was telling us over breakfast that there was a healthy population of blackcock on the shoot. Unfortunately, they were just out of season so we couldn't shoot one. I had never seen a blackcock so it was worth going for that reason alone.

We arrived about twelve and Sid introduced us to the owner. A well spoken young man who made us feel welcome. He had brought three friends with him from England for a few days shooting. The area that I saw consisted of part woodland and part moorland. We shot the woods first, splitting into two parties of four, standing and beating alternatively. It was hard going through the woods. They had never been thinned out and were full of briars. On one of the occasions I was standing, I saw Ian coming out of the side of the wood, totally exhausted. He was leaning against a tree, puffing and panting. The colour of his face was between crimson and blue and I was concerned for him. I thought he was going to have a heart attack. He got his breath back and stood up. Shaking his head as much as to say, I must be mad, he vanished back into the wood. The shooting was good with all the birds off wild stock. These birds had learnt the art of survival and it was entirely different to shooting reared birds. The birds were reluctant to fly, knowing they were safer on the ground. When a dog did manage to push them up, they flew like bullets.

After half a dozen drives through the woods we went to the moorland. I have never seen such uneven ground in my life. It was full of holes and outcrops of rock. The holes were full of snow and the rocks were slippery. I would have been better off with mountaineering boots on, rather than Wellington boots. We lined out across the moorland with the young owner on one end of the line and me on the other. Instead of walking it in a straight line, he issued the orders that we would wheel it round. If you have ever seen ice skaters being swung round the rink when they are on the end of a line, you will understand what I mean. The young man stood virtually still, while I was on the other end of the line, running up and down mini mountains with sweat pouring out of every part of my body. When birds did get up, the young man didn't miss many. I actually saw him miss a very high pheasant, with the wind up its bum, and he was really cross with himself. It's funny how people set different standards for themselves. I probably wouldn't have fired at it because it was too high for me.

Once we had stopped wheeling round and started to walk in a straight line, I started to enjoy it more. I enjoyed a couple of sporting shots at pheasants but it was a shame the blackcock were out of season because they were springing up within range. Sid told us later that when they are in season you can't get near them.

Later, we split up and went to three different duck ponds. I went with the young owner and one of his friends. They were keen shots. As soon as a duck appeared it was shot. They never waited for it to fly round or to see if there were any others following it in. I must admit they were good shots but far too keen for me. I soon realised I wasn't going to shoot the way I preferred to and put my gun in it sleeve. I watched them shooting and they just seemed to be obsessed with killing everything. *Lisa* enjoyed picking up for them. She brought me twelve mallard and four teal.

On the way back to the house which he called his shooting lodge, he asked me how many ducks I had shot. He had been so intense on his shooting, he hadn't noticed I had put my gun away.

We had a cup of tea and thanked him for the day, then went back with Sid for our dinner. Later when we were having a drink by the fire, I could hardly keep my eyes open. My legs were tired after running through the Himalayas for most of the afternoon. Sid told us he had arranged another trip for us the following morning with yet another keeper and produced another map of how to get there. I was soon in bed and didn't need rocking. Tony woke me at quarter to six. I had slept through my alarm.

We were driving towards Stranraer again but turned off before we got there. The fields were still covered in snow and it was another cold morning. We stopped in front of the keeper's cottage and were disappointed to find that there were five other wildfowlers waiting. The keeper eventually came out and told us to follow him. We walked about half a mile up a track and then into a field which had a ditch running down the side of it. We were walking along the side of the ditch when the keeper said, *"Someone in there!"* There was the usual courtesy of wildfowlers, pushing and shoving until one had jumped into the ditch. I heard the splash and was glad it wasn't me. We walked the full length of the field and the keeper positioned his guns at intervals in the ditch. I am not one for fighting for position, and found myself the only one left as we reached the far side of the field. The keeper said, *"Get in at the end."* This I did and was pleased that I had the dry end. I could hear the geese talking to each other not too far away. They must have been roosting on a loch. As it started to break light it became apparent why we were there. The field in front of us was full of kale about two feet high. It was probably the only food around that wasn't covered in snow. My lack of enthusiasm to fight other wildfowlers for an early position in the ditch had paid off. The geese started to fly in from their roost and they had to come past me first. The first skein of greylags came and I decided to let them past to give them a chance of a shot further down the ditch. The fellow next to me shot at them while they were out in front of me. I then realised what I was up against. I decided that I would shoot three geese and five minutes later I had them safely retrieved and lying next to me. I put my gun away and watched the carnage. There were far too many geese shot that morning. After about an hour the keeper blew his whistle for the shooting to stop. Everybody climbed out of the ditch and some of them started to walk among the kale to retrieve their geese. Like the keeper the morning before, he couldn't get us away quick enough.

Ian had shot two geese which he picked but Tony hadn't fired a shot. He was so disgusted with the two lunatics either side of him, he put his gun away early and watched. The geese were desperate for food and the keeper was exploiting this by filling the ditch with wildfowlers every morning and collecting ten pounds from each one. The following Monday, The Department of Agriculture & Fisheries put a ban on shooting wildfowl until there was an improvement in the weather. I hope the geese stripped the field of kale to the ground. We paid our ten pounds each and I vowed I wouldn't go out with a keeper again for geese. To this day I have stuck to that vow I made all those years ago.

When we returned to Sid's, we told him the story. Sid thought he had organised it just for us and didn't know anything about the other five guns.

After breakfast Sid asked us if we would like our last evening flight at Orchardton. He said we could split up. Two to the pond at the back of the wood, which we never shot last time, and two to the flash where I had shot the wigeon. Sid thought, with me and Alan leaving it early, there would have been a few more coming in that wouldn't have been frightened. I told him it would be a good way to finish off the week. He said, *"That's not the finish! Alan is coming over in the morning and we are taking you to Orchardton for the geese."*

When we had eaten breakfast I went to bed and slept until three o'clock. At three-thirty we were on our way again for the ducks. Sid took Ian to the pond behind the wood and Tony came with me to the mill pond which was more like a flash. The weather was different to the last visit there, with a sky full of thick cloud and a trickle of snow blowing in the air. We settled into the gorse bushes and the light was fading fast.

Lisa's tail started to wag, then the whistle of wigeon followed by the sound of rapid wing beats and a dozen wigeon were screaming over the flash. We fired almost together. with me taking one from the rear and Tony taking one from the front. There was no time to fire a second barrel. Sid and Ian fired several volleys on the other pond before we were in business again. It was nearly dark when I received the signal from *Lisa*. The wigeon took me by surprise as they came over me from behind. As I shot one they swung over Tony and he took another. I was having difficulty picking them out now, as they kept coming in. After three misses in a row, I decided to put the gun away. I watched Tony carry on shooting. I couldn't see the wigeon but I could hear them splashing down after they had been shot. Tony is quite deaf and doesn't have the pleasure of hearing them coming like I do, but I think there must have been an owl in his family tree, because he seems to be able to see in the dark. Ten minutes later we walked back to Sid's car. Ian and Sid were already there with four mallard and two wigeon. We had nine wigeon and Tony had shot seven of them.

It was our last night so after dinner we went to a pub in Newton Stewart. By the time we had drank three pints it was closing time at half past ten. The landlord bolted the door and came back behind the bar. I told him we were ready to leave. He looked quite indignant and said. *"What's wrong boys, have you ran out of money?"* I told him we still had some money left and he said, *"You better have another pint then!"* and proceeded to fill our glasses. We had to laugh at his cheek and managed to escape after we had drank the pint. The landlord couldn't understand us. He thought we would want to stay there until three in the morning. Maybe The Greg had been there before us.

When we got back to Sid's house he was still sat by the fire and poured us a night-cap. He told us that Alan had been on the phone and told him he couldn't come with us in the morning. He carried on to tell us the tactics for the morning. We were going to split up. He told us the geese nearly always flight off the bay over Orchardton but you can't be sure which part of the farm they will cross. He was taking Ian to one side and me and Tony were to go to the other side. Sid started to tell me the directions where to go. Maybe not the best time to tell me, because when I have consumed alcohol in any quantity, I see the funny side of everything. He stood up, leaned back, put one hand over his pouch and started to point, as though we were in the fields. *"You go across the first field, over a stile that's a bit rickety, across another field, keep in line with the 'tallywag poles.' You will come to two trees, one big one and one small one, go between them and head diagonally across the field, you will come to a gate with string on it. Go through the gate."* I was totally lost by now, so I interrupted him to jokingly ask him what colour the string was. He said, *"I think it's red but it could be blue!"* We burst out laughing and couldn't stop. I don't think Sid realised what we were laughing at. He soon realised he couldn't get any sense out of us so he decided to write it down on a bread wrapper. I was still giggling in bed until the alcohol took over and I went out for the count.

Up early the next morning with a sore head but I still had a smile on my face. We arrived at Orchardton and parked at the back of the farm buildings. Climbing over a stile into a field we split up to go our separate ways. It was pitch black and I couldn't see my hand in front of me, never mind a row of 'tallywag poles'. With map and torch, we set off in the direction that Sid pointed, walking through frozen snow. After wandering around in fields for half an hour looking for markers on the map, we did eventually arrive at the place we were supposed to be. Standing behind a stone wall we waited for the day to break. I started reflecting back on the week.

How fortunate we had been to find a person like Sid. Nothing was too much trouble for him. I have had good accommodation before but I have never met anyone who organised so much shooting for us with no financial gain for himself. He is a truly remarkable and knowledgeable man who enjoyed talking about the shooting as much as doing it.

As the day started to break I could see the layout of the land. We were on high ground with five fields in front of us sloping down to the foreshore. Wigtown Bay was still, with patches of soft low cloud gliding slowly across it. The A75 ran along the shore line on the opposite side and the lorry headlights hardly seemed to be moving. It was such a peaceful moment I shall never forget it. What a privilege just to be there! I could hear geese a long way away. Just a muffled noise as though they were still chatting at their roost. Three hares were running around in the field in front of us, stopping to scratch in the snow to expose something to eat. What a hard life these wild animals have during a cold spell!

It was half past eight and full daylight when the geese decided to move and what a magnificent sight it was. They lifted up somewhere near South Balfern and flew along the bay towards Orchardton. Skein after skein lifted, following the same flight line. From our elevated position we were looking down on them. The sun had popped up and was reflecting on the still water. As they came closer the noise became louder and louder. There must have been well over two thousand geese in the sky, stretching two miles down the bay to South Balfern. As the first skein swung right to come over Orchardton, more skeins were still lifting from their roost two miles away to add to the continuous line. I have never witnessed anything of this magnitude. The first skein flew over me and Tony, sixty yards high. I dropped a net over my face so I could look up and enjoy this spectacular show. Skein after skein followed the line, right over the top of me. The show lasted for twenty minutes and then they vanished into dots in the distance. It's a wonder that *Lisa's* tail didn't fall off. Some of the later skeins were probably in range but we never bothered to shoot. It would have been a shame to break up the convoy. They seemed to know where they were heading. I hope it wasn't that kale field.

Our last breakfast at Sid's was more than we could eat. He was determined to fill us up for our long journey back. After breakfast I gave the truck a quick wash while the boys were sorting out the geese and ducks we were taking back with us. Sid took quite a few to distribute to his farmer and dairymen friends who had been kind enough to allow us on to their land. The truck had served us well. It was just a few months old and not a mark on it. I stood back and admired it with its gleaming blue paint.

I unlocked and lifted up the flap of the hidden compartment under the flat bed back and put the key in my jacket pocket. We then started the task of carrying everything down the stairs and packing them into the compartment. After about five trips I started to get warm and took my jacket off, placing it by the front wheel of the truck. We stacked everything in and I said I would go back to the rooms and check that we hadn't left anything. The rooms were clear and when I went outside to tell the boys I was horrified to see Tony pushing my jacket into the compartment. As I shouted, he slammed the lid down and it locked.

The luck of the Raw strikes again. The keys for the truck are locked in the compartment. We tried to pick the lock and tried other keys that Sid had, but without success. The only thing to do was to cut the hinges. I borrowed a hacksaw from Sid and it broke my heart to cut into the blue shiny hinges of the flap. I cut a slot in them managing to prise them open enough to release the pins attached to the flap. Pushing my hand in I pulled out the coat. I had to use a hammer to close the hinges up again. We laugh about it today but I wasn't very pleased at the time. Tony had seen the coat by the wheel and thought it had to go under the flap with the rest of the gear.

As we were about to leave, we were sitting in the cab and Sid was stood there with a smile on his face, leaning back with both hands protecting his tackle. I said to him, *"Your directions were not very good, Sid. That bloody string on the gate was actually white!"* We all had a good laugh and headed back to the rat race.

Alan Dimmock was one of life's gentlemen. He became a very good friend and I knew him for twenty years with fifteen of them spent living in Scotland just a few miles from him. In all that time I never heard Alan say a bad word about anyone. When I was moaning about some idiot, he would tell me to be more tolerant with people. He always saw the good side of people without looking for the bad. Tragically Alan passed away in 1998 and is sadly missed by us all. He loved the countryside and the shooting scene and it was a privilege to be associated with him. I have some wonderful memories of a man I respected and they will never fade.

There are many more stories which cover three decades of wildfowling. I visited Sid for five years. There were five more trips to Islay and numerous trips to The Wash and the Ouse Washes where we stayed in the cabin. If we had been wealthy we could have bought the perfect boat for our trips to the Ouse Washes but that would have spoilt the fun. We had to make do with what we had and it was tremendous fun trying different methods of beating the elements. We even cut the roof off an old van, turning it upside down we carried out some modifications and called it 'The Factory Ship.'

After going through a divorce in the early eighties I married Jennie and we have lived by Wigtown Bay for the last fifteen years. She is a wonderful lady and accepts the fact that I am mad and understands my love of the foreshore. I was a member of the small Orchardton syndicate for a number of years and learnt a great deal about the habits of the geese. There are many stories I could relate, like my youngest son Stuart, who was twelve at the time, shooting his first goose with a twenty bore, after I had crawled the length of four muddy fields to put the geese over him.

I will include them in my next book, *"On the Flight Again!"*. Stories taken from my treasured diary and a head full of wonderful memories.

e-mail gallowaycottages@aol.com